England's Abbeys

MONASTIC BUILDINGS AND CULTURE

England's Abbeys

MONASTIC BUILDINGS AND CULTURE

PHILIP WILKINSON

ENGLISH HERITAGE

Published by English Heritage, Isambard House, Kemble Drive, Swindon SN2 2GZ
www.english-heritage.org.uk

English Heritage is the Government's statutory advisor on all aspects of the historic
environment.

First published 2006

10 9 8 7 6 5 4 3 2 1

ISBN-10 1 85074 944 2
ISBN-13 978 185074 944 8

Product code 51006

British Library Cataloguing in Publication data
A CIP catalogue for this book is available from the British Library.

Edited and brought to publication by René Rodgers, English Heritage Publishing
Designed by George Hammond
Indexed by Alan Rutter
Printed in the United Kingdom by Bath Press

FRONTISPIECE:
Whitby Abbey at sunset.

Contents

Introduction

OR ALMOST ONE THOUSAND YEARS, from the 7th century to the early 16th, there were monasteries in Britain. They did not flourish for this entire period. There were times of decline, for example during the Viking raids of the 9th century. And there was a sudden and painful end, when Henry VIII closed all the monasteries in the 1530s. But by the time Henry dissolved them there were hundreds of abbeys and priories up and down the country, home to thousands of monks and nuns. They prospered for long enough to leave one of the most striking and fascinating architectural legacies in Britain.

You cannot travel far in England or Wales without encountering some sort of evidence of a medieval monastery. Many former monasteries are ruins, left to decay after the dissolution. Some were converted to a different use – numerous country houses, such as Forde Abbey or Nostell Priory, and smaller houses, such as Denny Abbey, were built by cannibalising the remains of a medieval monastery and some still preserve remnants of the monastic buildings amongst their halls and drawing rooms; others have been rebuilt and their origins survive only in their names. Many farms incorporate former monastic buildings in their barns or cowsheds. Sometimes an abbey or priory church was taken over by the lay population and remains in use as a parish church. Occasionally the buildings have disappeared, but a memory remains in the form of a street name such as Priory Road or Abbey Terrace.

OPPOSITE PAGE:
The ruins of the church of the Cistercian abbey at Byland.

At Lacock Abbey, the remains of the Augustinian nunnery were converted to a private house in the 16th century.

This huge variety of remains and echoes can make medieval abbeys difficult for the modern visitor to understand. Apart from the fact that most of these buildings are fragments of what they once were, there are several other reasons why they can be hard to fathom. First, the monasteries were dynamic institutions – ideas and ideals about the monastic life changed as time went on and the buildings changed too. Second, the way of life of the monk or nun is remote from modern experience. Third, monasteries were amongst the most complex structures of the Middle Ages. It is the aim of this book to unravel some of these issues, to help visitors understand the ruins better and enjoy them more.

CHANGING PATTERNS

From the earliest centuries of the Christian era there were two main ways in which a person could live a monastic life. The first was the way of the hermit, the man or woman living a life of prayer and devotion alone; the second was the way of the monastery, where the devotee lived in a communal monastic setting. This is the way of life that had such an enormous influence in the Middle Ages and is the subject of this book.

A fragment of a 12th- or 13th-century tile from St Augustine's Abbey, Canterbury, bears the image of a monk.

Monks and nuns promised to give up family ties, personal property, relations with the opposite sex and countless freedoms that lay people take for granted, and to devote their lives to God. In the Middle Ages Christianity was at the heart of everyone's life, the church was one of the most powerful of all institutions and nearly everyone saw their time on earth as a prelude to an afterlife. A life devoted to God was therefore attractive to many. Some saw it as a vocation, the ideal way of being a pious Christian. Others regarded it more as a job, a chance for people – especially younger sons who would not inherit their parents' property – to pursue an interesting and possibly influential career.

Thus monasteries attracted many recruits and many different characters. The life of a monk or nun was a hard path to follow and some fell short of the ideal. The historical record is full of accusations that monks did not take their vows seriously enough – they ate too much, talked too much, left the abbey precinct needlessly or did not attend church as often as they should. Complaints like this inspired calls for reform, for a return to monasticism's basic values. And every so often a dynamic churchman would start a new monastery run along different – and usually stricter – lines. If successful, the new house would inspire the foundation of daughter houses and a new order or monastic movement would be formed.

A monastic order was a distinct group of religious houses, following their own rule (often a version of the most important monastic document, the rule of St Benedict of Nursia) and with their own system of organisation and government. By the end of the Middle Ages there were numerous orders of monks and nuns in Europe, but a handful achieved special success and popularity in England. In addition to the original Benedictine monasteries (not formally an order but similar to each other in outlook), the Cluniacs, Cistercians and Carthusians were the most prominent orders of monks in England and Wales. The orders of canons – particularly the Augustinians, Premonstratensians and Gilbertines – were also widespread. Later the friars – notably the Franciscans and Dominicans, who also followed a monastic rule but were very different in their outlook, lifestyle and goals from the monks – came to prominence.

Many of these orders accepted women and set up separate establishments for them. There were Benedictine and Cluniac nuns, Augustinian and Gilbertine canonesses, and sisters who were allied to the orders of friars. Other orders, such as the Cistercians, did not accept nuns into their ranks and so there were generally fewer opportunities for women to join monasteries.

However, the orders were not quite as hard and fast in their make-up as this suggests. There was nothing to stop an aristocrat founding a monastery for a group of women who wanted to follow the Cistercian way of life. They might even call themselves Cistercian, even though they were not actually part of the Cistercian organisation.

But fluid as they were in some ways, the different orders of monasticism developed their own ways of life and sometimes their architecture reflected this. Cistercian abbeys have a slightly different plan from Benedictine houses and the Carthusian monasteries have a radically different layout from either. Cluniac monasteries were often lavishly decorated, while Cistercian buildings tended to be more austere, and so on.

A reconstruction of Kirkham Priory shows the prior's hall as it was in the 14th century.

THE MONASTIC LIFE

For all their variety, some key precepts underlay the life of every monk and nun. Each took vows of poverty (renouncing personal property of all kinds), chastity and obedience. They usually lived in virtual silence. They wore the standard costume, or habit, of the order. They were confined, for the most part, to the abbey precinct. Again, there were exceptions to this. A monk who was in charge of abbey farms might have to travel and talk much more than his brothers. The friars, too, were notable travellers, teachers and preachers. But all lived under strict vows that set them apart from the rest of society.

If monks and nuns lived a life apart, they also found themselves in many ways at the heart of medieval society. This seems like a paradox, but would not have seemed so in the Middle Ages. The bulk of the monastic day was taken up with the liturgy – with prayer and reciting the psalms. This activity in itself was central to medieval life – everyone believed in God and the afterlife. Monastic prayers paid special attention to the monastery's lay benefactors, so monks and nuns were providing a

This piscina, a basin for washing sacred vessels, is set in a decorated niche at Cleeve Abbey.

special service through their prayers, effectively reducing the amount of time the benefactors would spend in purgatory.

Monasteries provided many other services. They gave alms and assistance to the poor and needy. They sometimes provided accommodation for the elderly. Many monks and nuns were skilled in healing the sick. Monastic infirmaries were mainly for the monks and nuns themselves, but monasteries also ran hospitals for lay people and monastic nurses or physicians were no doubt consulted by lay people on occasion. As major landholders, abbeys were responsible for maintaining law and order on their estates and so held courts and punished wrongdoers. As custodians of holy relics and shrines, abbeys attracted visitors and set up guest halls and inns for travellers.

Monasteries were also centres of education and scholarship. In order to learn and understand the words of their prayers, psalms and sacred readings, monks and nuns had to be literate and they passed their literacy on to the young people who joined the monastery. When they were not in church, many spent their working hours writing – before the

St Augustine's Abbey, one of the most important early monasteries in England, is shown in this reconstruction as it would have been in the 16th century.

invention of printing with movable type, nearly all books were written and copied in monasteries. Furthermore, the skills of the literate monk could lead him beyond the cloister. A number of monks who rose to the rank of abbot became the trusted counsellors of kings, sometimes travelling on diplomatic work or drawing up treaties.

In the early Middle Ages, abbeys influenced education still further – pupils from outside the cloister were also taught in monastic schools. This practice died out by the 11th century, with cathedrals and charitable schools taking over this role. But some abbeys still supported schools: Augustinian canons taught in schools in both Oxford and Cambridge, and some of the charitable schools were later put under the aegis of their local abbeys. When the friars arrived in Britain, they were enthusiastic teachers, once more contributing to the development of the universities.

At a more mundane level, many monasteries were like large businesses. Most abbeys held land and property. Some of the land provided food for the inhabitants of the monastery, some could be let to tenants to provide an income to pay for necessities that could not be made in-house or provided by benefactors. In the process, some monasteries became rich and influential. They were not always the isolated communities that they seem when we look at their ruins today.

The 14th-century fish house at Meare provided a home for the water bailiff of Glastonbury Abbey and rooms for drying, salting and storing fish from the nearby lake.

And this is not surprising, because in the Middle Ages monasteries were an important part of the social system. In general, the eldest son inherited the family house and land; younger sons often had to make their own way. One way was through the church and therefore many aristocratic younger sons became monks. In the abbey they would get an education and the chance to rise to the position of prior or abbot, or to find a vocation as an ordinary choir monk. Daughters – whether they had a true religious vocation or simply could not find a husband and the security of marriage – might also enter a nunnery. As a result, most upper-class families had a link with at least one monastery.

Abbeys also needed workers, people who were employed to do the jobs around the monastery that the monks and nuns could not do or had no time for, from building maintenance to work on the abbey farm. This gave members of the lower social classes a role in the monastery. In the Cistercian order male workers could even become members of the monastery – known as lay brothers – though they had a lower status than full choir monks.

Thus, by the 12th and 13th centuries and through the rest of the Middle Ages, the monasteries were affecting all classes of society, were widely scattered across both towns and countryside, were providing numerous social services and were central to religious life.

ABOUT THIS BOOK

Monasteries were important in the Middle Ages, but why should we care about them today? First, they have left behind buildings and ruins of remarkable interest and beauty, traces that have inspired Romantic poets, film-makers, historians, artists and the countless visitors and modern pilgrims who still flock to see them. Second, they form a unique window on to the medieval world. An understanding of monastic ruins can lead to an understanding of medieval religion and much more: the diet, agriculture, industry, art and thought of the Middle Ages. To grasp how they worked, it helps to know something about both their history and their architecture, as well as about the individual monasteries themselves. To this end, this book is divided into three main sections.

The first section provides a short history of the development of monasticism, tracing its early origins in the Middle East and its history in England and Wales from the first Christian missionaries in the Saxon period until the monasteries were dissolved by Henry VIII in the 1530s. Each of the main orders is introduced at the point in the story when they arrived in Britain, so this is the place in the book to look for information about the characteristics, lives and values of the principal orders. This section casts its net wide, including in its coverage of monasticism the friars and the military orders, groups of men who followed a rule, but who lived a life sometimes far removed from that of the cloistered monk. It also addresses the development of nunneries.

The second section covers the main buildings and features of a medieval monastery, describing what each part was like and how it was used. It examines the monastic church, the domestic rooms such as the refectory and dormitory where the monks or nuns ate and slept, the working buildings dotted around the monastic precinct and some of the structures, such as farms and town developments, built by the monks outside the precinct on their outlying lands.

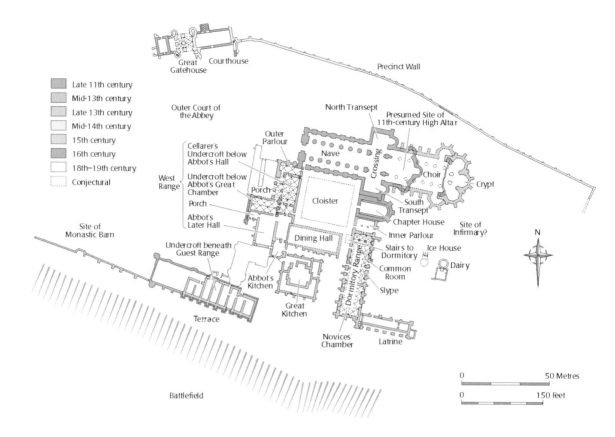

Late 11th century
Mid-13th century
Late 13th century
Mid-14th century
15th century
16th century
18th–19th century
Conjectural

Great
Gatehouse
Courthouse
Precinct Wall

Outer Court of
the Abbey

North Transept
Presumed Site of
11th-century High Altar

Cellarer's
Undercroft below
Abbot's Hall

Outer
Parlour

Nave

Crossing

Choir

Crypt

West
Range

Undercroft below
Abbot's Great
Chamber

Porch

Cloister

South
Transept

Porch

Abbot's
Later Hall

Chapter House

Site of
Infirmary?

Site of
Monastic Barn

Inner Parlour

Dining Hall

Stairs to
Dormitory

Ice House

Undercroft beneath
Guest Range

Dormitory Range

Common
Room

Dairy

Abbot's
Kitchen

Slype

Great
Kitchen

Terrace

Novices'
Chamber

Latrine

N

Battlefield

0   50 Metres

0   150 Feet

This plan of the abbey at Battle illustrates a typical monastic layout.

The third section is a gazetteer. It covers most of the monastic sites in England and Wales where there are substantial remains and a number where the remains are slight but interesting. It includes ruined sites, monastic churches still in use and monastic buildings that were converted and given a new life after the dissolution. It is not intended as a substitute for the excellent guidebooks available at many monastic sites, but provides a quick summary of the kinds of buildings that a visitor can expect to find.

A note on terminology

Several different words are used to describe monasteries and nunneries, and appear in the names of the buildings. Most common are abbey and priory. An abbey was the name used for a major or independent monastery, ruled by an abbot. Benedictine abbeys were normally independent houses, Cistercian abbeys were answerable to the mother house of the order at Cîteaux. A priory, headed by a prior, was usually a monastery that was dependent on or founded from another house. Priories were thus often smaller than abbeys, but this was by no means always the case. Cathedral-monasteries were generally referred to as cathedral-priories and all Cluniac monasteries, large and small, were referred to as priories, because all were dependent on the main house of Cluny. Friars were based at friaries. More information on the terms used to describe monasteries, those who lived in them and the life they led can be found in the glossary at the end of the book.

A sense of grandeur was often the first impression produced by a medieval monastery and gatehouses, like this one at Battle Abbey, could be among the grandest of all monastic structures.

The development of monasticism

OPPOSITE PAGE:
A typical Norman doorway, decorated with chevron moulding, leads into the nave of Lindisfarne Priory.

T O MODERN EYES there is something alien about the monastic life. Walling oneself off from the rest of the world and renouncing private property, luxury and the company of the opposite sex seem the reverse of what most people want. But people did not always see things like this. The 12th-century historian Gerald of Wales, describing the early Welsh monasteries of Bardsey and Beddgelert, wrote that the monks devoted their lives to the service of God, 'living in a holy and common bond, having nothing private, in the manner of the Apostles'. In other words Gerald saw that the monastic life has some of its origins in the lives of the Apostles themselves, at the beginnings of Christianity. But monasticism itself was born slightly later.

It seems to have begun in the 4th century AD in the Middle East. At this time many Christians were becoming hermits, choosing a lonely and self-denying life in the desert to try to get back to the basics of their faith. But a Coptic Christian and former Roman soldier, Pachomius (c 292–346), chose a different path. Pachomius had been a hermit. He had been attracted to many aspects of the hermit's life, which freed one

BELOW LEFT:
This reconstruction shows St Cuthbert's hermitage on Inner Farne in around AD 686.

BELOW RIGHT:
Part of a 10th-century cross shaft from Lindisfarne, carved with a figure that may be Christ in Judgement, reflects the kind of art produced in the later Saxon era.

from worldly distractions and gave one the time and space to pray, meditate and, it was hoped, reach spiritual fulfilment. But Pachomius saw that this ascetic way of life – known as the eremitic lifestyle – was not for everyone. The hermit was isolated and had no support. Pachomius realised that a religious community – still isolated and ascetic, but providing mutual assistance – was the answer. So, around AD 320 he founded the first true monastery at Tabernisi in Upper Egypt. There he developed a communal Christian way of life, known as the cenobitic lifestyle, from the Greek *koinos bios*.

Pachomius saw that his followers needed a practical and moral framework to guide them in their new life. He developed a rule by which he and his followers lived. It covered the key aspects of the life of the monk – his work, his religious observance, his poverty and his obedience to the head of the community, Pachomius himself. It was a harsh way of life but it proved popular. There were nine monasteries and two nunneries in Egypt by the time Pachomius died in 346.

Pachomius's original monastery was a large community – one authority says that there were 1,300 monks living there. They lived in a walled precinct that contained a church, a dining hall, a building for guests and a number of houses, each with accommodation for some 20 monks under the supervision of a prior.

The cenobitic way of life developed by Pachomius was enormously influential on later monasteries. The communal emphasis, the rule, the hierarchy, the importance of obedience, the value set on work, the regular worship – all these elements were picked up by the founders of later monasteries, spreading the monastic ideal around the Middle East and beyond. The regime followed in these early monasteries, constantly adapted and reformed, influenced monks and nuns for centuries.

Other church fathers helped the cause and development of the monasteries. One of the greatest was St Basil of Caeserea (c 330–79), a bishop who cemented the connection between the monasteries and the rest of the organised church. Basil was also a notable writer and his ideas about the importance of work and obedience were very influential. He is regarded as the father of monasticism in the Orthodox Church, and the monks of the modern monasteries on Mount Athos and at Meteora in Greece are his heirs.

THE SPREAD TO THE WEST

But how did monasticism come to the West? First of all, the writings of
the early churchmen spread the idea of the monastic life far and wide.
Many of their works were biographies of the church's desert fathers –
both hermits and cenobitic monks – that gave a clear idea of the actual
flavour of the life of the monastic pioneers. Once these works were
available in Latin – the language of the church and of scholarship in
Europe – they were widely available and widely read. St Jerome
(*c* 341–420), a scholar who wrote numerous lives of the church
fathers, also translated Pachomius's rule into Latin.

Another early biography, the *Life of St Anthony* by St Athanasius
(*c* 296–373), patriarch of Alexandria, was also much read in the West.
It told the story of another Egyptian Christian who, like Pachomius,
founded a monastery. St Anthony of Egypt – healer, scholar and
gardener – was a popular saint. But, like Pachomius, he was a rather
remote figure to Europeans. For monasticism to thrive in Europe, a
founding father from closer to home would be helpful. That figure was
one of the most influential of all monks, St Benedict (*c* 480–*c* 550).

Not much is known about Benedict's life. He was born in Nursia,
Italy, and studied in Rome before becoming a hermit at Subiaco. Soon he
attracted disciples and he began to organise them into a formal
community. But at some point there were difficulties with the locals at
Subiaco – someone is rumoured to have tried to kill Benedict – and he
moved to Monte Cassino, near Naples, where he put the finishing
touches to his rule, a document that would eventually be followed by
thousands of monks and nuns.

Benedict's rule drew on the previous monastic rules, but was more
comprehensive, more practical and better organised than its
predecessors. It defined the main activities of the religious life (liturgy
and prayer, sacred reading, manual work) and it made clear the moral
precepts by which monks and nuns should live (such as humility, poverty,
chastity and, above all, obedience). It discussed their training and laid
down instructions about daily life, indicating the amounts of time the
monk or nun should spend sleeping, reading, eating and so on. It
considered monastic discipline. It specified how abbots should be chosen
and what the qualities of a good abbot should be (wisdom, learning and

An image from the 11th-century
Eadui Psalter *shows St Benedict*
giving the rule to his monks, while
the scribe Eadui kneels at his feet.

discretion were important virtues, but the abbot should also be a father figure for his community). And it was full of advice and instruction about running the monastic community and its spiritual life.

The rule was demanding, but it was also practical. Benedict knew that the monastic life was not for everyone – but also that it could be very attractive. Therefore he did not make it easy to be admitted to a monastery as a full monk or nun. A new brother or sister had to be sure of their vocation. Because of this, a candidate, or postulant, had to ask for admission repeatedly, over a period of several days, before being admitted. And even then they were let in only as a novice. A year's novitiate had to be served, to allow for the appropriate training, education and preparation for the full monastic life, and to enable waverers or those who did not turn out to be suited for the monastic life to turn away.

Benedict's rule eventually guided the lives of thousands of monks and nuns. Benedict did not intend to found an order of monasticism, whose members would look on him as a leader. He was a practical man, laying down the guidelines for his own community. But the rule was so comprehensive and so useful that it was taken up widely. It was also attractive because it was unusually well written. The text is full of succinct phrases and epigrams, such as 'Idleness is the enemy of the soul' and 'Let nothing have precedence over divine service.' Such phrases indicated straight away the priorities of the monastic life. And Benedict's viewpoint was completely that of the cenobitic monk. Though he did not mean to write propaganda, the rule was an excellent advertisement for the monastic community as opposed to the life of the hermit. The influence of St Benedict was powerful and his name stuck. In later centuries, followers of his rule would become known as Benedictines.

THE FIRST BRITISH MONASTERIES

Monasticism probably came to Britain and Ireland during the lifetime of St Benedict, in the last quarter of the 5th century, though we cannot be sure of this. But we do know that Palladius, a churchman who probably came from Auxerre, was sent as bishop to the Irish Christian community in 431 and that he was succeeded soon afterwards by St Patrick (385–461), a British priest, who established his headquarters at Armagh. Where there were Christians, there were soon monasteries. Christian leaders such as St Columba (521–97), founder of monasteries such as Derry, Durrow and perhaps Kells, and St Finnian (*c* 495–579), founder of the monastery at Clonard and many others, were especially influential. During this period numerous monasteries and hermitages were founded in Ireland, many on the remote islands and crags of the west coast.

Irish monks travelled to Scotland, bringing the monastic life with them. For example Columba and 12 others went to Iona, off the south-western tip of the Isle of Mull, in 565, where they founded the most famous of all Scottish monasteries. Cormac, an associate of Columba, founded a still more remote community on the small rocky island of Eileach an Naoimh off Jura. Many other island monasteries were beginning in Scotland at around this time, both in the Western Isles and on the mainland.

In Wales there were major monasteries at St David's and Llantwit Major by the 7th century, as well as many smaller houses. Bardsey, an island off the Lleyn Peninsula, was said to be home to the first religious house in Wales. Another very early site was Beddgelert in Snowdonia. By this time there is also evidence for dozens of monasteries in south-east Wales, especially along and near the valleys of the Wye, Monnow and Usk rivers. We know about these not from remains but from charters, and if there was more documentary evidence from the rest of Wales we would probably know of many more early houses.

These early foundations were part of the process by which Britain was converted to Christianity. In England the groundwork was done mainly in the 7th century and missionaries moved across the country in an unconscious pincer movement. Members of the Northumbrian church moved southwards, while churchmen such as St Augustine of Canterbury (died *c* 604) established the faith in the south, moving gradually outwards from bishoprics at Rochester, London and Canterbury.

Despite having similar aims, the two arms of the pincer were rather different in character. Augustine was a monk, Italian by birth and sent from Rome by Pope Gregory the Great in 597. He worked from his base at Canterbury, in the monastery of St Peter and St Paul, which later became known as St Augustine's. From here he sent out missions to the southern Anglo-Saxon kingdoms and, as kings and queens were converted to the new faith, they too founded monasteries. Backed by the

This artist's impression shows the Rotunda, a round building constructed to link two churches on the site at St Augustine's Abbey. It was built by Abbot Wulfric just before the Norman Conquest.

pope and spearheaded by Augustine, who knew Rome well, these new foundations were heavily influenced by the Holy See. They laid heavy stress on the communal monastic life and many probably followed St Benedict's rule. It is likely that an Italian monk would have felt at home in the monasteries founded by Augustine and his colleagues.

It was slightly different in the north. St Aidan (died 651), an Irish monk and colleague of St Columba from Iona, was the founder of the first Northumbrian monastery, located on Lindisfarne or Holy Island. He was sponsored by Oswald (c 605–42), king of Northumbria, who had converted to Christianity when in exile at Iona. Soon Aidan was founding other monasteries in Northumbria and instituting reforms such as freeing Anglo-Saxon slaves and educating them so that they could become monks.

Aidan's Celtic origins meant that his brand of monasticism was also Celtic. The monasteries were more like group hermitages, whose inhabitants lived a less communal life than those in the southern houses. There would be separate cells within a precinct for the monks, who aspired to a stricter asceticism than their Roman counterparts. A monk might even retire periodically to live apart as a hermit – something that

St Aidan was the leader of the first monks at Lindisfarne. His mission was to convert the people of northern Northumbria to Christianity.

The church at Jarrow has a Victorian nave and Norman tower, but parts of the chancel (on the right of the picture) belong to the Saxon monastery where Bede lived.

St Cuthbert (*c* 634–87) did – before returning to the monastic precinct.

Thus there were two strains of early English Christianity, but they were not as far apart as one might think. Some of the northern abbots travelled widely and were well connected with Rome. The historian Bede (673–735) was educated by Abbot Benedict Biscop (628–89) at Monkwearmouth and by Ceolfrith (died 716) at Jarrow. Bede tells us much about Biscop, a nobleman who gave up a life serving his king to become a monk. Biscop was a cosmopolitan character. He became a monk at Lérins Abbey on Ile de Saint-Honorat and visited Rome several times. On one occasion he returned from Rome with a large collection of books and a prominent Roman monk, John, abbot of St Martin's in Rome. John taught the Roman liturgy and Roman script. Biscop was also briefly abbot of St Augustine's Abbey in Canterbury.

The career of Benedict Biscop shows how close England's two churches could come and how the Northumbrian church in particular could combine Roman and Celtic ways. It was a rich mixture that produced Bede's writings (including his *Ecclesiastical History of the English People* and *Lives of the Abbots*) and many fine illuminated manuscripts. The early church produced many monastic buildings too, but these have almost completely disappeared as the result of demolition and rebuilding. But the surviving archaeological evidence suggests that these early monasteries consisted of a number of isolated buildings set rather informally around one or more churches. The foundations of such buildings have been excavated at a number of early monastic sites, from Whitby in Yorkshire to St Augustine's in Canterbury.

DECLINE AND REVIVAL

The early abbeys were successful but fragile. They relied on good leadership and a peaceful society. In the later 8th century, the British monasteries, no longer led by inspirational abbots like Biscop, were in decline. Then peace was also threatened. The monasteries came under attack in the raids of plundering Vikings. By the 9th century many monasteries had been pillaged or burned to the ground and their monks were scattered or worse. A revival was due, but new foundations needed powerful patrons.

The monasteries found champions in several English kings, beginning with King Alfred (reigned 871–99). Alfred is the only English king to be known as 'the Great'. Originally king of Wessex, he fought and then made a treaty with the Danes and eventually ruled a united England. He was literate and had visited the pope in Rome as a boy. This background showed him the importance of encouraging monasteries and education, and he laid the foundations of a monastic revival in England. This revival came to fruition under Alfred's successors in the 10th century: Edmund, Eadred and, most importantly, Edgar (reigned 959–75), a young, well-educated ruler who gained a reputation as a lawgiver and who encouraged cooperation between church and state.

One of the key monasteries in this 10th-century revival was Glastonbury. A monastery had existed there at least since 601, but its importance was due to the appointment of Dunstan (909–88) as abbot in 940. Dunstan, a local man of noble birth who had been educated in the monastery, proved a dynamic leader. He introduced the rule of St Benedict and inspired reforming zeal in his monks, but faced a setback when a dispute with King Eadwig forced him into European exile in the late 950s. Abingdon was another important centre of monastic revival under its abbot, Aethelwold (c 912–84), a friend of Dunstan's. A further centre was Westbury on Trym, near Bristol, the monastery of Oswald (died 992), a monk who had previously been a canon of Winchester.

These three dynamic church leaders enjoyed additional support when Edgar came to the throne of Wessex in 959. Dunstan was welcomed back from exile and was appointed archbishop of Canterbury. He returned well informed about monastic ideas across the Channel and keen to spread

The abbey of Glastonbury was vast and only an aerial view of the fragmentary ruins gives some idea of the sheer scale of the site.

ideas of monastic reform in his new province. He also persuaded the king to appoint Oswald as bishop of Worcester. Aethelwold, meanwhile, was made bishop of Winchester.

All three new bishops used their power and influence to encourage the monks of their former monasteries to found new reformed monastic houses. Soon monks from Glastonbury were spreading to other houses in the south and west, while Glastonbury itself expanded. The abbeys of Malmesbury, Bath, Athelney, Muchelney and Westminster all benefited from this reforming influence. From Westbury, monks spread to found houses such as Evesham, Pershore and Ramsey. Altogether some 50 monasteries were either founded or refounded in the 50 years after Edgar came to the throne. A number of these were based on lands given by the king himself.

In each case these monasteries followed the rule of St Benedict, but under Dunstan's influence they modified their daily ritual and routine to bring it in line with the best practice in Europe. Aethelwold saw the need to rewrite the rule to take account of these changes and in about 970 he produced the *Regularis Concordia*, a monastic law code that set down a basis for religious observance and was, again, founded on St Benedict's rule.

Dunstan, Aethelwold, the other leaders of the 10th-century monastic revival and their followers promoted the importance of work – both manual labour and the intellectual labour of writing and copying books – in the life of the monastery. Many of the monks were notable scholars and at this time, as in the rest of the Middle Ages, this meant being fluent in Latin, the language of intellectual life throughout Europe. But in England, the monks also had notable writers in their mother tongue. King Alfred had inspired them through his actions: the king himself translated historical works into Old English, commanded other translations to be made and instigated the writing of the *Anglo-Saxon Chronicle*, a history of events in England covering the years AD 1 to 1154.

The foundations of the Saxon church at Muchelney Abbey lie within the larger footings of the later medieval church.

Another prominent man of letters was Aelfric (died *c* 1010), a pupil of Aethelwold, who ended his life as abbot at Eynsham in Oxfordshire. Aelfric was the greatest prose writer of the Anglo-Saxon period. His *Catholic Homilies* and *Lives of the Saints* were widely read and his other works included a translation into Old English of the first seven books of the Bible. His Old English style – elegant, rhythmic, alliterative, but also clear – is still appreciated by scholars. A keen educationalist, Aelfric also compiled a Latin grammar, his most popular book in the Middle Ages.

One of the greatest promoters of Old English was St Wulfstan (*c* 1008–95), a monk who, during a long life, was bishop of London, Worcester and York. Wulfstan wrote sermons in Old English, one of which includes an account of the damage caused by the Viking raids. As a senior churchman and royal adviser he also compiled law codes for both King Ethelred and King Cnut.

These two learned monks were very different characters. Aelfric lived the quieter life as an abbot, but was eminently practical, writing in Old English to reach a larger audience and appealing for the proper education of young people so that they might grow up to be wise teachers in turn. Wulfstan was a master of rhetoric, not afraid to use his eloquence to denounce the sins of his flock. He was also successful in the church hierarchy, a holder of important bishoprics that took him close to the crown.

The revived monasteries of the 10th century looked to the king for protection. This was significant, because it reduced the influence of local lay lords over the monasteries. In the liturgy the importance of the king was confirmed with the addition of prayers for the royal family. This kind of link between political and religious institutions, between the church and the monarchy, is something that remained a key aspect of medieval life. The church had a political role and the crown a religious aspect.

England's rulers in the decades before 1066 kept up this tradition of encouraging the monasteries. King Cnut was a supporter, as was Edward the Confessor, who rebuilt Westminster Abbey and whose queen, Edith, helped to rebuild a nunnery at Wilton. At this time there were many abbeys and they held a huge amount of land; if some of their leaders, such as Wulfstan, could have a huge influence on the monarchy, the king in turn often expected to have some influence over the choice of abbots.

Therefore, by the eve of the Norman conquest, many of the English monasteries were revived, reformed and powerful. They were centres of learning that had produced important manuscripts – from the sermons of Wulfstan and Aelfric to non-religious works such as the *Anglo-Saxon Chronicle*. Some of them occupied substantial buildings. They were numerous, held much land and kept a close link with the monarchy.

At Deerhurst the west wall of the nave has a two-light window, a strange triangular opening, and a round-headed door, all remains of the Saxon monastic church.

THE NORMANS

William I (reigned 1066–87) acknowledged the importance of the church and he sought its approval for his actions before conquering England. Afterwards, he oversaw the gradual replacement of Saxon abbots and bishops with Normans. This did not happen overnight. Most of the Saxon abbots carried on in office until they died – the exceptions were mostly those implicated in plots against William. Thus there was a gradual shift, as steadily more and more Normans assumed charge of monasteries up and down the country.

Meanwhile, as if to signal a further change in the fortunes of the church, the Normans embarked on a huge rebuilding programme. Parish churches and cathedrals were rebuilt as well as monasteries, many of the wooden churches of the Saxons being replaced in stone. These Norman buildings – with round-headed windows, doors and arches, thick walls and an increasing amount of ornate carving – proved durable buildings. Though they have mostly been much altered over the centuries, many still stand as testimony to the Norman commitment to the church.

In some ways, though, the conquerors left things as they were or even strengthened English traditions. For example they seem on the whole to have promoted local Anglo-Saxon saints, whose relics abounded in English and Welsh monasteries. When churches were rebuilt they reserved special places for these remains. And Norman monks continued the old custom of writing the lives of these local church heroes and heroines.

Another tradition that the conquerors encouraged was that of the monastic cathedral. When they arrived in England, four cathedrals – Canterbury, Sherborne, Winchester and Worcester – were also monasteries. The bishops of these cathedrals also had the title of abbot; the monks, governed by the prior, made up the chapter. This was a very English way of doing things, for in continental Europe monastic and cathedral churches were usually kept separate. But the Normans seem to have liked the system. After the conquest they established several other monastic cathedrals. Under the Normans, monks were sent to Rochester from Bec (the former abbey of Lanfranc, who was archbishop of Canterbury from 1070 until 1089); the secular canons at Durham Cathedral became monastic; cathedrals were created in the monasteries

The imposing twin western towers at Durham are a good example of the sheer scale of early medieval church building.

of Bath, Chester and Ely; Norwich Cathedral, a new foundation of around 1095–6, was monastic; and the Augustinian priory at Carlisle also became a cathedral in 1133.

This rash of monastic cathedrals involved a number of building projects. Winchester Cathedral was rebuilt by the Normans and its two transepts still display the round arches of the early Norman masons. Durham is one of the finest of all Norman churches. Its nave, noble in its proportions and ornate in its decoration, is one of the great spaces of English building. Norwich too has a stunning Norman interior. These were major buildings in some of the most important English cities. By building in stone and on a huge scale, these cathedrals were a statement of Norman power, as well as statements of piety.

The Normans did not stop at cathedrals. They proved to be notable founders of monasteries and, again because they often built in stone, their structures have survived in large numbers. These foundations could take various forms. Some were not independent abbeys at all, but were cells of an abbey in Normandy. An alien cell was a miniature monastery that was set up to manage lands in England that had been granted to a French monastery. Cells were often very modest, manned by a handful of monks from Normandy who lived in an establishment that probably resembled a manor farm next to a church. Alien cells were mainly economic foundations, existing to help houses manage their lands. To English people, they must have represented blatant land-grabbing by French monasteries and they were too small to put much back into the community where they squatted.

Rather more worthwhile were the dependent houses, small priories that were founded as subsidiary houses of already-existing monasteries in England or Normandy. Many of these priories were in Wales or along the Welsh borders – for example those of Abergavenny, Chepstow and Monmouth were dependent on abbeys on the other side of the Channel, while Brecon, Cardigan and Carmarthen were dependent on English abbeys. Unlike the alien cells, these dependent priories were proper monasteries. But they were small houses and most have left little trace behind them. Mick Aston, in his *Monasteries in the Landscape*, selects the priory church at Stogursey, Somerset, which has survived as a parish church, as a good example of a building in which the architecture reflects the priory's French origins. The ornate carvings on the capitals of the crossing piers are very like those on contemporary French churches.

Some of the new Norman abbeys were not dependent priories or alien cells, but were independent English Benedictine monasteries. The latter

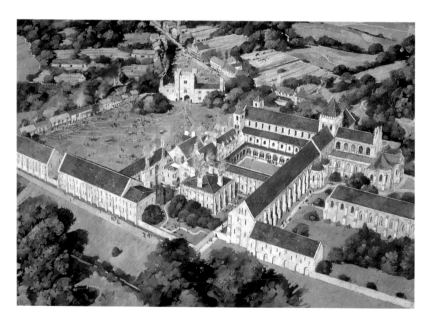

This artist's reconstruction shows Battle Abbey as it might have been in the early 16th century. Some Norman features, such as the nave with its row of single-light windows, can still be seen.

included Selby and, most famous of all, the abbey at Battle that was built after the battle of Hastings, part act of piety by William, part war memorial. Many such monasteries were in towns that also had Norman castles. By the end of the 11th century there were a number of these, such as Shrewsbury and St Nicholas's Priory. Aelfric's old abbey of Eynsham had also been refounded.

Many of the Norman abbeys were rebuildings of Anglo-Saxon foundations. These could be large buildings with big endowments. A look at two of the great Benedictine abbey churches of the west of England – Tewkesbury and Gloucester (now Gloucester Cathedral) – shows the scale they could achieve. Both churches, though much remodelled in later centuries, retain their big Norman naves, with rows of massive round drum-like piers. These are major buildings, symbolic of the huge confidence of the Benedictines in the years after the conquest – and of the vast resources that Norman patrons could sink into their buildings.

THE CLUNIACS

The magnificence of the great Benedictine buildings was not the end of the story. As the Norman period progressed, still more abbeys were founded. Some of these buildings were as magnificent and ornate as anything produced by the Benedictines and they belonged to a more recent order of monks: the Cluniacs. The Cluniacs favoured elaborate ritual and the finest in art, architecture and vestments, and they made a big mark.

The name of the Cluniac order comes from the abbey of Cluny, which had been founded by William, Duke of Aquitaine, in 909. The abbey, in a richly wooded valley in Burgundy, eventually grew to be the largest monastery in western Europe. In its final form, its architecture was stunning, with a collection of spires and turrets pointing to the sky. It was also the envy of many traditional Benedictine houses because of its independence – Cluny's charter gave it the right to choose its own abbots without the interference of lay patrons. By the time the Normans came to England, Cluny was already large and its influence was spreading.

The abbey of Cluny and its order were immensely influential partly because of the way they were organised. The monks were all considered

to belong to the mother house and their monasteries were all subsidiary
to Cluny and were all known as priories. These close links, together with
the Cluniac preference for fine architecture and ritual, gave the Cluniacs
a distinctive image that appealed to the Normans. It was an image that
they were familiar with, because scores of Cluniac monasteries had been
founded all over France before the Normans arrived at Hastings. Before
1100 a number of Norman-backed Cluniac monasteries were also
established in England.

The first was Lewes, which was founded by the Norman lord William
de Warenne (died 1088) in 1077. In 1089 Castle Acre was founded from
Lewes by William's son, another William (died 1138). Soon it was joined
by several houses founded from the French Cluniac monastery of La
Charité, notably Wenlock Priory. These links between monasteries were
not always close. The evidence is that the Cluniac order was rather
loosely organised – the distance between Cluny and the English daughter
houses made contact difficult. But it had a notable influence on the
architecture of the time and this can still be seen, even in some of the
English Cluniac buildings that survive as ruins.

The Cluniacs were a reforming order. They were founded partly in
response to the idea that many Benedictine monasteries had become lax
and corrupt. Therefore the Cluniacs aimed to follow the rule of St
Benedict more strictly. They believed that religious observance – prayer,
the divine office and the celebration of Mass – was far and away the most
important aspect of the life of the monk or nun. So the Cluniacs focused
on the liturgy – they celebrated Mass and the office in the most elaborate
way, spending more time on it than was usual in other monasteries.
They decorated their churches lavishly to provide a fitting setting for their
worship and they also adopted rich vestments.

Cluniac monasteries could be very impressive places, their churches
richly carved and glowing with candlelight and the colours from stained-
glass windows. The perceived piety of their monks attracted many lay
donors and Cluniac monasteries were able to acquire costly decorations
and precious relics. These well-endowed houses became highly effective
advertisements for reformed monasticism.

What was more, Cluny's founding fathers ensured that the order
remained free to foster their holier, more liturgy-centred way of life with
a minimum of local interference. Duke William of Aquitaine insisted that

the monastery should be free of feudal obligations – the monastery did not owe any dues to the founder and the founder could not interfere with the running of the abbey. Cluny was to be subject only to the pope, meaning that even local bishops could not interfere, as they often did with Benedictine houses.

In spite of the order's freedom from interference and the benefactions it attracted, the Cluniac monasteries in England could not compare in size and wealth with the oldest and largest of the Benedictine houses. British Cluniac abbeys tended to be smaller than the major Benedictine foundations. But their numbers multiplied. Lewes was followed by Bermondsey, Castle Acre, Pontefract, Thetford and Wenlock, together with Cluniac nunneries at Arthingon and Northampton.

The life of the monks and nuns in these houses was conditioned by the Cluniac enthusiasm for the liturgy. They spent most of their time in church or in private prayer. Little time was left for the other main elements of the monastic life: manual work and study. To do the manual work, most Cluniac priories employed servants, much as the Benedictines did already. The exceptions were the smaller houses, which often did not have the resources to pay for house servants – here the monks had to do much of the work themselves. Cluniac monks were less famous for their learning than their Benedictine counterparts. Even so, many Cluniac monasteries had sizeable libraries, with books covering a range of subjects from religion to history and law. Monks and nuns with a special skill in writing or scholarship were sometimes allowed to spend less time in church than their fellows so that they could work in the scriptorium, the area of the abbey dedicated to the production of manuscripts.

By the 12th century, many monks had flourished under the Cluniac system and some of the most influential clergy in England were Cluniacs. For example Henry of Blois, who was bishop of Winchester from 1129 to 1171, was one of the most powerful men in the country – he was the grandson of William I and the brother of King Stephen (reigned 1135–54), and he supported the king in his struggle for the throne against the Empress Matilda. Henry was the most influential churchman of his time, becoming papal legate (representative of the pope) in England in 1139. When Henry put his weight behind Stephen's cause, the other bishops followed. It was an important step in tightening

Stephen's grip on the throne. As well as being an example of Cluniac power, Henry was also said to be a good bishop, working for the benefit of his diocese and founding St Cross, a hospital in Winchester.

The way the Cluniacs governed themselves was radically different from the way previous abbeys were run. Each monastery was founded from a parent house and remained dependent on this parent. Each parent was in turn dependent on Cluny, whose abbot was the sole authority of the whole Cluniac community. In other words, the Cluniacs were the first true monastic order – they were unified by a hierarchical organisation as well as by their common belief in the prime importance of the liturgy.

The abbot of Cluny was the pivotal person in the order. It was his job to maintain discipline by visiting each of the order's houses in turn. Clearly, as the order grew and monasteries multiplied, this became more difficult. This was especially the case in England, since the monasteries here were far away from Cluny itself and visitations were rare. This situation could pose problems. For example, when an abbot died, the head of Cluny was not always available to choose a new one. In England when this happened, the monks would sometimes ask the abbot for permission to appoint a new person from amongst their ranks or to promote a monk chosen by the abbey's patron. And so the order's very success, leading to its spread across Europe, could also lead to interference of the very kind that it tried to discourage.

Interlaced arcading on the north wall of the chapter house at Wenlock Priory represents Cluniac design at its richest.

At the Cluniac priory of Castle Acre a fine Norman west front stands next to the much later prior's lodgings, an indication of the high standard of accommodation enjoyed by many priors of the order.

Distance could also pose a challenge when it came to discipline. If a monastery stepped out of line, it was the responsibility first of the mother house, and then of Cluny itself, to bring it back in step. But mother houses were often far away and Cluny, in the heart of France, was a vast distance from any English house. Therefore Cluniac monasteries were often far more independent than the order's founding fathers intended.

The progress of the Cluniacs was modest in England, but they left behind some impressive remains. In the ruins of Wenlock Priory, for example, are the finely carved walls of a chapter house that must have been one of the most magnificent rooms in Norman England. The gatehouse at Thetford and the west front and prior's house at Castle Acre are amongst the glories remaining to evoke the Cluniac order and its love of creating the most appropriate settings for the worship of God.

THE CISTERCIANS

Soon after the Cluniacs were established in Britain, the Cistercian order was founded in France. The Cistercian order – named after its mother house at Cîteaux in Burgundy and destined to be even more influential than the Cluniacs – began in 1098 as a group of monks who wanted to find a new way of getting back to the basics of the monastic rule. They wanted a more austere way of life, without the distractions of the lavishly decorated Cluniac monasteries or the temptations posed by the easy life found in many Benedictine houses. So they developed a harsher, more stringent regime and developed a system of government to keep it in place. In doing so, they became one of the most successful of all the monastic orders.

The Cistercians arrived in England in 1128, when a group of monks settled at Waverley in Surrey. But the big step for the English Cistercians was the foundation of a number of large monasteries in Yorkshire. The first of these were Rievaulx and Fountains, both founded in 1132; others followed as the new order began to dominate the spiritual life of the north and to play an increasing part in the region's economy.

The cellarium, or store room, is one of the surviving buildings at the Cistercian abbey of Waverley.

Rural Yorkshire suited the Cistercians ideally. They did not want wealth and thus rejected the temptation to accept rich cultivated manors or rights over mills, fisheries, fairs or other gifts from which they could derive an income. Instead, the Cistercians wanted isolation. They were content with previously uncultivated land on which they could farm sheep and keep at a distance from worldly concerns. Soon they were farming large areas of Yorkshire and building huge monasteries that still survive as vast and evocative ruins.

Here they could live a life truly apart from the secular world. They rejected comfortable clothes, lavish vestments and rich decoration in their buildings – such as paintings, wall-hangings, stained glass and carpets. They wore simple, undyed habits, which earned them the nickname 'white monks'. Their altars were plain, without hangings and with a simple wooden cross. They kept candles and lanterns to a minimum. They turned away from the Benedictine habit of accepting oblates, infants who were given to a monastery by their parents and allowed no choice in whether or not to follow the life of the monk. In their religious observances they did away with elaborate processions, kept chanting to a minimum and had few special services. This freed up time for work and study so that the Cistercians could get back to an appropriate balance of the three main elements of the monastic life – liturgy, work and scholarship.

The Cistercians also tried to impose austerity from the top down. Their abbots were encouraged to live a life as frugal as that of any other monk in the choir and they had few officials. A Cistercian, first and foremost, was a monk and did not expect to leave behind the simplicities of the monk's life if he was promoted to become the leader of his house.

To make this regime work, the Cistercians devised some changes to the old monastic order. Most fundamental of all was the fact that the Cistercians were the first monastic order to have a written constitution.

A row of round Norman arches bridges the aisle at the vast Cistercian abbey of Fountains.

This document, called the *Carta Caritas* (*Charter of Charity*), guided the way each monastery was run and defined the organisation of the order as a whole.

Another major change instituted by the Cistercians was the annual general chapter, at which all the abbots of the order met to discuss business and discipline. Then there was the order's system of visitations. Instead of the visitations by the local bishop usual in Benedictine abbeys, Cistercian monasteries were visited from their mother house. The visitor had specific duties, which were set down in writing. He was to investigate the abbey's observance of the liturgy and the monks' conduct in a range of areas from their observation of the rule of silence to their diligence in caring for the sick. He was also empowered to enquire about the abbey's financial health. Each monk could meet the visitor in private to talk through any specific problems or grievances. The visitor could sack officials if they were not doing their job properly, but could not remove an abbot without first taking advice. His findings were written down, deposited in the abbey and read out periodically in chapter to remind the monks of the areas where improvement was required.

A further innovation transformed the inner workings of every Cistercian monastery. To help with the work of field and farm they established a new category of members, the *conversi* or lay brothers. Lay brothers were the manual workers of a Cistercian monastery. They spent most of their time in the fields, the mason's yard or the workshop of the blacksmith or carpenter. Many worked in outlying farms, known as granges, where they were supervised by a senior lay brother called a grange master. Granges were a key element in the large farming enterprises of the Cistercians. They sometimes also fulfilled other functions, such as offering hospitality to travellers.

The lay brothers followed a quite separate vocation from the choir monks. They were usually illiterate and were never 'promoted' to the choir, but lived the life of the craftsman or farm worker all their lives. Spending most of their time working, the lay brothers said a simpler form of the office than the choir monks. Their presence meant the choir monks had more time for liturgy and study as well as a certain amount of manual work – usually lighter tasks such as gardening or working in the kitchen – when required.

Tiles from the refectory at Cleeve Abbey bear the arms of Richard of Cornwall, a notable 13th-century patron of the Cistercians.

To modern eyes this system, with its notion of two 'classes' of monks, may seem exploitative of the lay brothers. But in medieval terms it opened up the monastic life to a new group. Previously, monks had come mostly from the educated upper classes – a monk needed to be literate to study. Now a young man from the peasant or labouring classes could become a lay brother and dedicate his work to God.

In the 12th century, the Cistercians proved immensely attractive to prospective brothers – the stress laid on simplicity and austerity seemed to offer a better, more rigorous form of monasticism than that available in the older monasteries and it caught on. It was also attractive to lay people who wanted to found a religious house. The fact that the Cistercians were a reforming order with a clearly austere lifestyle was in their favour. So was the fact that they preferred 'waste' lands that no one else wanted to cultivate. Their abbeys proliferated, especially in Yorkshire where there were eight monasteries, but they were also dotted about many other parts of the country.

At the Savigniac abbey of Furness, an ornate arched doorway leads into the chapter house.

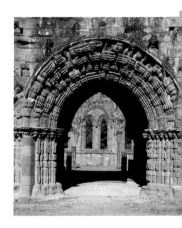

The Savigniac order, named for its mother house in France, aspired to a purity similar to that of the Cistercians. But it was not as well organised and there were tensions between the order's different monasteries. By the 1140s there were 14 Savigniac monasteries in England and Wales, most founded directly from Savigny but a few, including Byland and Calder, founded from Furness. In 1147 there was a dispute in the order about whether Byland should be dependent on Furness or Savigny. This was not the only argument about the governance of the different Savigniac houses, and such arguments made it difficult for Serlo of Savigny, the head of the order, to keep effective control. So in 1147 Serlo sought union with the Cistercians, who gave permission at their general chapter that year.

However, the process of union was not straightforward. The monks of Furness opposed the move, sensing that their influence would be lessened. And many Savigniac houses did not live up to the austerity of the Cistercians. Sometimes, as at Swineshead, Cistercian monks had to be sent to a former Savigniac house to instruct their colleagues in the way of life of the white monks.

To some the Cistercians must have seemed formidably austere, but their ranks had room for men of great humanity, characters such as Ailred (1110–67), a priest from Hexham who became a monk at Rievaulx

Some of the walls of the church at Rievaulx still stand almost to ceiling height, supported by graceful Gothic arches.

in 1134. Ailred found favour both because he coped well with the harsh Cistercian regime (in spite of poor health) and because he dealt well with people. He served as his abbey's envoy to Rome and then as its Master of the Novices before being appointed abbot of Revesby Abbey in Lincolnshire in 1143. In 1147 he was recalled to be abbot of Rievaulx. With Ailred as leader, the abbey prospered, attracting some 140 monks and around 500 lay brothers. There were also several daughter houses. His inspired leadership and numerous writings – including a treatise on friendship – showed the human face of the Cistercians.

As time went on, the temptation to exploit other kinds of income proved irresistible to the Cistercians. They began to acquire villages, mills, churches and other properties that brought in regular money and soon many were landlords on as large a scale as the old Benedictine abbeys. As a result, throughout the 14th and 15th centuries they came to rely less and less on farming their own lands and the numbers of lay brothers decreased. Eventually, most abbeys did without lay brothers; their accommodation – which had usually been built along the western range of the cloister – was given over to other uses. A number of 14th-century Cistercian abbots built themselves lavish quarters on the site of their monastery's old lay brothers' wing. Meanwhile, the lay brothers' area in the church was cleared of their stalls, freeing up space for processions. And so, towards the end of the Middle Ages, the Cistercians began to look less distinctive than they had been.

The remains left by the Cistercians are some of the most beautiful of all monastic ruins. They are often in isolated rural spots and are commonly built in an austere but well-proportioned kind of Gothic architecture that lends them a special character. A rare surviving Cistercian church that still stands roofed and in use is the one at Dore Abbey, where the eastern section is used as the parish church. With its pointed Gothic arches and simple vaults that embody a chaste beauty, it gives a good idea of the kind of building in which the Cistercians worshipped.

The surviving church at Dore Abbey consists of the transepts, chancel and east end of the original Cistercian abbey church.

The other major English medieval Cistercian sites are ruins. But their beauty frequently takes the breath away and it is no accident that Tintern, the abbey that inspired one of Wordsworth's most famous poems and began the Romantic tradition of venerating ruins, was a Cistercian house. The finest sites, especially Rievaulx and Fountains, are enormous, with extensive standing remains of churches, domestic buildings and the ancillary structures used in the day-to-day work of the abbey. They have provided archaeologists with some of the best evidence of the growth and use of medieval monastic buildings and no doubt still have many more secrets to reveal.

THE CARTHUSIANS

The Cistercians breathed new life into monasticism by trying to get back to the simple basics of the communal lifestyle. The Carthusians, another group that began in this period, took a different direction, combining the communal life with some aspects of the life of the hermit. In the process, they created one of the most widely respected of all the monastic orders.

The Carthusians began in 1084 when St Bruno (*c* 1032–1101), a canon and teacher from Reims, set up a small community of hermits on a mountainous site given to him by the bishop of Grenoble. Here Bruno and his followers built huts in which to live, following a stark regime of prayer and silence. In 1142 they became a formal religious order based at this original settlement, which was called La Grande Chartreuse (The Great Charterhouse).

The monks of La Grande Chartreuse lived much of the time in their individual cells, where they studied, prayed and recited most of the canonical hours of the divine office, meeting in church only for matins, lauds and vespers (*see* p 75). They ate the simplest food, wore the coarsest clothes and soon acquired a reputation as the most austere of all monastic communities. An early account of the monks' lives described how each week they received enough bread and vegetables for the next seven days and how each monk would cook this food in his own cell. It recorded how their church was plain and unadorned, with precious objects shunned except for a single silver chalice.

The order expanded, with new houses following a similar regime, but the growth was slow. St Bruno and his colleagues realised that their austere life was not for everyone and they put a formal brake on growth – each new charterhouse was to have only 12 monks and a prior, plus a community of up to 18 lay brothers.

The first Carthusian monastery in England was established at Witham in Somerset in 1179. Henry II founded it as an act of atonement for the murder of Archbishop Thomas Becket by his men in 1170. Witham's first two priors were undistinguished men. They only managed to build a few wooden huts on their site and the small number of monks who lived there struggled to survive. In spite of the harsh conditions, they were also

This is the living room of a reconstructed Carthusian cell at Mount Grace Priory.

failing to achieve one of the main aims of the order – isolation – because some 120 peasants were living nearby. Everything changed with the arrival of the great churchman Hugh of Avalon (*c* 1140–1200), who came from La Grande Chartreuse in 1180 and stayed as prior of Witham for four years. Hugh immediately tackled the issue of the peasants. With the backing of the king, he bought up their houses and they were given new homes and land on the royal manors of their choice. Hugh thrived at Witham and soon the monastery was thriving too, attracting distinguished monks to the small community.

But Henry II had a different role in mind for Hugh – the king wanted him to be bishop of Lincoln, the country's largest diocese at that time. Hugh resisted, but the head of La Grande Chartreuse agreed with Henry and so Hugh moved. In Lincoln he was a notable bishop, reviving the schools, rebuilding the cathedral and defending oppressed minorities such as the Jews. He helped make the Carthusians famous for learning, piety and justice.

The English Carthusian community remained tiny, with houses at Hinton and Beauvale, founded in 1232 and 1320 respectively. But in the later 14th century, after the devastation caused by the Black Death (1348–50), a flurry of further charterhouses was founded as the result of patronage by the royal family and the higher nobility. Thus the London Charterhouse (1371), and those at Hull, Coventry, Epworth and Mount Grace, came into being.

It is interesting that these noble and royal patrons turned to the Carthusians when they wanted to found monasteries in the late 14th century. This was a time when there were few new monasteries, the country had been hit by the Black Death and the monastic ideal in general was less popular than it had been 200 years before. It says something about the reputation of the order that these foundations could come about in this context. With time for reading and private study, they produced their fair share of devotional writers, whose works demonstrated the continuing thought and piety of their order. The ruins of Mount Grace Priory stand as the most evocative medieval reminder of the lifestyle that fostered such piety. But modern Carthusians still remind us that their order has never been reformed because it has never needed reforming.

THE REGULAR CANONS

The church had included canons amongst its clergy for centuries. Canons were normally bodies of clerics who served a large church such as a cathedral or minster. They lived communally, eating in a refectory and sleeping in a dormitory, and were paid from the treasury of the church. These men were secular canons – they did not live according to a monastic rule as monks did. Frequently they left the communal life to occupy houses belonging to their church; sometimes they even married and raised families.

During the 11th century there was a movement in the church to reform these bodies of canons by encouraging them to be celibate and to follow a rule, amongst other provisions. Those who took this path were known as the regular canons. They followed a rule that was based on one of the letters of the great bishop and theologian St Augustine of Hippo (354–430), which he had written to the members of a religious foundation in North Africa. As a result, these regular canons came to be known as the Augustinian or Austin canons.

On the whole the rule of the Augustinian canons was slightly less restrictive than that followed by the traditional monks. They spent rather less time reciting the office and they were allowed more freedom when it came to conversation and travel. These differences were appropriate since the canons were priests who ministered to the lay people who came to their church. Some were also appointed vicars of other parish churches. And others served hospitals, curing the sick in a number of towns and beginning the foundations that became London's St Thomas's and St Bartholomew's hospitals. As a result of these activities, the lives of the canons could be more outward-looking than those of traditional monks.

The Augustinian canons came to prominence in England in the early 12th century. From the beginning, they benefited from royal support, especially from Matilda, queen of Henry I. Matilda founded an Augustinian priory in Aldgate, London, a house that rapidly created several new Augustinian establishments. The king himself endowed the Augustinian abbey at Cirencester. From bases like these, the Augustinians expanded rapidly and in a few decades they had more than 100 abbeys and priories dotted around the country.

Round, Norman-style piers line the ruined nave of St Botolph's Priory, the first Augustinian priory in England.

Augustinian priories were many and varied. The order had houses in both towns and villages. Some of their monasteries were large, but many were small, scattering the canons all over the country. As a result they became widely known and their buildings and remains, from country sites such as Lanercost to urban monasteries in cities such as Gloucester and London, are still thick on the ground.

The Augustinians were not the only group of regular canons established in Britain, though they were easily the largest group. There were also canons of the order of Arrouaise (which began at an abbey of the same name in France), of the Victorine order (from the abbey of St Victoire in Paris) and of the Premonstratensian order (from Prémontré near Laon, again in France). Of these, the Premonstratensians were by far the most successful in England. They arrived in 1143 and soon had 31 abbeys and 3 nunneries. Known as the 'white canons', from the colour of their habit, they were an austere group, owing something to the Cistercians (including the custom of holding general chapters) and, like them, tended to settle in remote country areas.

In addition to these groups was the one native English order, the

The early 16th-century tower is the most substantial survival at the Premonstratensian abbey at Shap.

Gilbertines, who were founded in 1131 by Gilbert, priest of Sempringham in Lincolnshire. Gilbert (c 1083–1189) set up his order at the behest of a group of seven women, who wanted to become nuns but had no nunnery to join. Gilbert built them a convent next to his parish church. Later, when the house had attracted more benefactions, Gilbert rebuilt his monastery as a double house, with canons and nuns living and working side-by-side. The canons acted as priests for the nuns and, as with the Cistercian model, there were also lay brothers and sisters to do much of the manual work.

In spite of the unusual arrangement that allowed canons and nuns to live together – albeit in separate buildings – the Gilbertine order had a reputation for propriety. Gilbert himself was an austere character and did not want to found an order of his own. He would have preferred to hand his monasteries over to the Cistercian order, but the Cistercians did not want a new batch of monasteries, especially since they contained women and Cîteaux did not normally admit nuns to its order. Therefore Gilbert was persuaded to keep his monasteries independent, forming their own, uniquely English, order.

The Gilbertines were never a large order (there were ultimately 24 monasteries in all, many in Gilbert's native Lincolnshire), but they proved popular. One reason for this was that they ran hospitals to care for the sick and homes for orphans, charitable work that was highly valued at a time when there were no central social services. Today the Gilbertines seem like an interesting footnote in the history of English monasticism, but to the people of medieval Lincolnshire, they must have held out a lifeline.

THE BENEDICTINE TRADITION

While the new orders were founding their abbeys and establishing their presence in Britain, the old Benedictine houses continued. Not formally constituted as an order, they were simply foundations that followed the rule of St Benedict in the traditional way, wearing the familiar dark habit that earned them the nickname 'black monks'. They were distinctive in some deeper ways from the new orders, but the degree of difference varied, because some Benedictine houses, especially the newer ones, fell under the influence of the more recent reforms.

The 13th-century west front at Tynemouth Priory is an elaborate Gothic design with many niches, one of a number of additions that were made to this Benedictine monastery.

One important way in which the Benedictines stood out was their relationship with their patrons. A Benedictine abbey traditionally had a feudal relationship with its patron, rather like the relationship between a lay tenant and his overlord. In other words, the abbey held its property in return for granting the patron certain privileges. In particular, patrons expected to enjoy the abbey's hospitality and to have some influence over the choice of the abbot.

The abbey might also hold property by military tenure, providing a number of knights to fight for the overlord in return for the use of the land. Since a monastery obviously had no direct access to fighting men, the abbey would therefore allocate some of the land to lay tenants, who would provide the knights for the overlord. The remaining land could be farmed directly by the monks. Later Benedictine foundations were often more independent, but even here a patron might expect to hold some sway over the selection of the abbot.

Another activity for which the Benedictines were known was the preservation of holy relics and the promotion of pilgrimage (*see* pp 89–94). Many Benedictine houses kept shrines containing relics and gained financially from a steady stream of pilgrims. One way of making money that was especially frowned upon by the other orders was the sale of indulgences. In return for a donation, pilgrims were offered an assurance that their sins were forgiven, so an indulgence was seen as a fast track to salvation. For many of the newer orders, the sale of indulgences was a clear example of the way in which the Benedictines had become corrupt.

The acceptance of child oblates was a further Benedictine custom that drew much criticism from reformers. Child oblates, entrusted to the abbey by their relatives, had no choice about whether to join the community. New orders such as the Cistercians rejected this practice, insisting that a novice should be free to choose whether or not to become a monk. As a result of this, the Benedictines, too, accepted fewer and fewer oblates until the custom died out. They still took in child novices, but these young people were, in theory at least, free to return to secular life if they felt that the monk's vocation did not suit them.

The balance of liturgy, work and study stressed by the rule was skewed in some Benedictine monasteries. Frequently, manual work was downplayed and servants were employed to do the heavy labour that was needed. The positive side of this failing was that Benedictine abbeys tended to allow more time for study and some were renowned for their learning, producing notable scholars and collecting large libraries of books.

There was no spiritual gain, however, in another of the Benedictine's failings – their modifications to the usual frugal monastic diet. The biggest loopholes came in the form of additions to the diet: these included the often lavish fare on the abbot's table and also the pittances – the foods, helpings and extra courses that were served to the monks at various times and on frequent feast days. The black monks were widely criticised for their rich diet though, as with all their failings, they were not consistent throughout the order. Some abbeys no doubt kept strictly to the rule, some flouted it continuously.

THE FRIARS

The 12th century saw a number of attempts to reform monasticism. Someone contemplating life in the cloister could choose between a traditional Benedictine house, the rural life of the Cistercians, the inward-looking, austere way of the Carthusians or the more outward-looking regime of the canons. But at the beginning of the 13th century there were still many who were dissatisfied with the monastic orders as they stood. The Benedictines in particular were still wealthy and had a reputation for bending the rule. The Cistercians too, with their large abbeys and big estates, looked increasingly rich.

There was room for another alternative. So it appeared, at least, to two visionaries of the early 13th century who wanted to truly embrace poverty and to serve God. They began a religious movement that not only embraced poverty more fully than before but also trained some of the most formidable intellectuals of the Middle Ages. The first was Francis of Assisi (c 1181–1226), a young man from a rich Italian family who had begun a military career, but had turned instead to the religious life. Francis gathered around him a group of 11 followers. They renounced all personal property, preached and cared for the poor and sick. In 1210 Francis drew up a rule and got it approved by Pope Innocent III and, with it was born the first order of mendicant friars, who refused to own property and supported themselves by begging. They eventually became known as the Franciscans. Two years later he founded a parallel order for women, under the leadership of St Clare; they would become known as the 'Poor Clares'.

Francis was a mystic. He received on his body the stigmata, the marks of the wounds inflicted on Christ at the crucifixion; he preached to the animals and birds; he insisted that he wanted to follow no rule except God's. He did not want to found a religious order, but, through his piety, integrity and single-minded devotion to his principles, he attracted so many followers that the formation of the Franciscan order became inevitable.

At around the same time a Spanish Augustinian canon, Dominic de Guzman (c 1170–1221), began to preach to the heretics in southern France. He also attracted followers, embraced poverty and found the approval of Innocent III and his successor Honorius III. Dominic's Order of Friars Preachers, later known as the Dominicans, was founded in 1216. Dominic saw that if they were to argue doctrinal points with heretics, his friars had to be well educated. He developed a regime in which the observance of the canonical hours took less of the day than in a normal monastery, so that his followers had plenty of time for study.

The 15th-century friary tower at Richmond in North Yorkshire is one of the few extant Franciscan examples.

Logic and theology became bread and butter to the Dominicans – they were well schooled to win arguments and well equipped to educate others. They became a formidable intellectual force.

Both orders of friars grew rapidly and they were joined by other orders, such as the Carmelites (also known as 'white friars') and Austin friars. This success was partly because the friars offered a fresh alternative for those seeking a religious life and, to many people, seemed to embody a more genuine return to the basic values of monasticism, especially concerning poverty, than the conventional orders. And their success was partly because their work of preaching and healing took them to the towns, which were changing quickly in the early 13th century.

Europe's towns were growing in this period. Populations were increasing, as was trade, and many towns were prospering as never before. Educational standards were also improving, mainly because most towns of any size had at least one monastery. And as a result of these developments, the people of the towns were alert, interested in spiritual matters, but also ready to criticise the monks of the traditional orders if their standards fell behind what was expected.

Thus the time was ripe for the arrival of the friars. Towns housed a growing audience for their sermons and a body of potential new recruits.

The nave, crossing and chancel of the Dominican church at Gloucester Blackfriars were much altered between the 13th and 16th centuries.

And in crowded medieval towns, news of the friars' work travelled fast.
The first Franciscans and Dominicans – known respectively as the 'grey'
and 'black friars' from the colour of their habits – arrived in England in
the 1220s and made straight for the towns. From Canterbury and London
they travelled to major cities such as Norwich, Bristol, York and especially
the university towns of Oxford and Cambridge. And as they spread, they
acquired new recruits, bringing ever-increasing strength to their
movement.

In the beginning the friars were not always well received. When they
arrived in a town there was sometimes friction with the local abbey,
whose abbot might see the newcomers as rivals. At Bury St Edmunds,
for example, the monks managed to keep out the friars completely.
Elsewhere, established monasteries resisted the friars but eventually had
to give up when lay patrons or churchmen gave the newcomers
somewhere to settle.

And so the friars established themselves in England, finding places to
live and, thanks to both parishes and the universities, platforms on which
to preach and teach. The royal family was also helpful, giving the friars
many donations and sometimes employing them on diplomatic
missions, for which they were well suited because they were both
educated and seasoned travellers. By the mid-13th century the Franciscans
and Dominicans had founded about 70 friaries between them and they
were soon joined in some places by the other mendicant orders. Soon
eleven towns had four friaries, one for each order, and many other towns
had two or three. It was a major religious movement.

The friars were impressive in their poverty. The Franciscans were
especially assiduous in this. They lived on alms but would not accept
money. They travelled barefoot in all weathers. They had only a single
habit with a cord girdle and one pair of breeches. The Dominicans were
less austere – for example they were allowed to wear shoes – but still
lived a simple life. The friars made many conventional monks look well
provided for and, ironically, this obvious poverty must have encouraged
the benefactions and legacies that eventually made the orders of friars
much less poor.

Francis and Dominic had forbidden their followers to own property –
the idea of renting land or houses to generate an income was anathema
to them. In the beginning, they were even uneasy about putting up

At Gloucester Greyfriars the spacious friary church was largely rebuilt in the early 16th century.

permanent buildings in which to live. In some places they made do with mud huts for years and in others they were unwilling to build churches of their own to begin with – often they were allowed to use a local parish church to celebrate Mass and the office. But soon the friars acknowledged that they needed bases – friaries with churches where they could preach and rooms where they could meet, study and sleep. These buildings were held in trust for the friars by the people of the towns where they settled. A rich citizen would often give the friars a house and act as trustee.

The friars were not interested in property and their domestic buildings did not have to conform to a standard monastic plan – they fitted in with whatever was available, often adapting existing buildings for communal use. Therefore surviving friary buildings are rather varied, though they have a few features in common, including spacious churches for preaching, good libraries and adequate space, often with individual cubicles, for study. Friary buildings are also rather rare, perhaps because, occupying city centre sites, they have mostly been recycled and rebuilt many times since the Reformation. So friary buildings have to be sought out – often a small medieval fragment survives in a back street somewhere; more often still evidence for a friary persists in a street name like Blackfriars. Only one friars' church has survived complete – the Dominicans' church in Norwich (now St Andrew's Hall) – though the towers of friars' churches can be see at King's Lynn and Richmond, North Yorkshire, and give one an idea of the beauty and sophistication of their architecture. Otherwise, the most extensive remains, encompassing parts of both church and ancillary buildings, are at the Blackfriars in Gloucester.

Oxford was one of the Franciscans' most important bases. Here they were encouraged by Robert Grosseteste (*c* 1175–1253), Chancellor of the University and famed as a teacher, and the friars themselves were soon well known for the quality of their teaching and scholarship. They eventually became as famous for their intellectuals (men such as Roger Bacon, Duns Scotus and William Ockham) as for their work in teaching the poor.

This tendency was just one aspect of the way the friars developed in general. The more they settled down, the more their lifestyle diverged from the original idea of wandering, preaching and begging. Their wealth was swelled by legacies and donations, and their begging became resented – especially when there were territorial disputes between different groups of friars about who was allowed to beg where. Specialised beggars known as limitors, who leased the right to beg on behalf of a particular friary and aimed to make a profit from their begging, were one abuse of the system. But the friars brought new life to monasticism in the 13th century and were good for the intellectual life of the towns and universities.

THE MILITARY ORDERS

From a modern point of view, the notion of a military order or a 'fighting monk' seems bizarre. The life of the soldier and the life of the monk appear at opposite poles. But to the medieval mind they were not so far apart – the knight saw his job in a Christian context, after all. And the idea of the holy war – especially the crusades in the eastern Mediterranean, which had the aim of wresting biblical places such as Jerusalem out of non-Christian hands – was familiar to all.

The military orders were set up in the context of the crusades. There were several orders, but two in particular spread to England: the Knights Hospitaller and the Knights Templar. The Hospitallers (more formally the Knights of the Hospital of St John of Jerusalem) were the older order, founded in 1092 when they established a hospital in Jerusalem to provide succour and hospitality for pilgrims on their way to Jerusalem. The Templars began in 1118, to defend the Holy Sepulchre in Jerusalem and to guard pilgrim routes in the Holy Land. Both orders took religious vows

but fought as knights and took a major part in the wars between the European Christians and the Egyptians and Turks.

Both military orders attracted donations and became rich. The Templars set up their English headquarters in the Temple in London, where their church – the Temple Church – still survives, its circular nave paying architectural homage to the Holy Sepulchre. The Hospitallers' English headquarters were also in London, at St John's Priory in Clerkenwell. Both orders also held a large number of estates around the country and though few of their buildings remain, their names often remain enshrined in local place names such as Temple Bruer and St John's Wood.

In the early 14th century there was a crisis in the military orders. The Templars, who had inspired jealousy because of their wealth and power, were accused of corruption and heresy. In 1312 the order was suppressed by the pope and most of its property was transferred to the Hospitallers (the crown acquired the Temple Church). Like the conventional religious orders, the Hospitallers survived in England until the dissolution of the monasteries in the 16th century.

The fighting monks were usually men from the upper classes, because for some of their life at least they would play the part of the knight. Membership of a military order opened up an interesting career, which could involve serving in one of the order's castles in the eastern Mediterranean, fighting on the Christian side against the Muslims and returning home to manage one of the order's estates or run one of its hospitals.

ABOVE LEFT:
The round nave of the Temple Church in London is the best-preserved English church of the Templars.

ABOVE RIGHT:
Tombs of Templar knights are arranged across the floor of the Temple Church.

There is still a scattering of remains of the Templars and Hospitallers on the ground in Britain. Other notable buildings include dovecotes and domestic buildings. In addition, great barns like the two at Temple Cressing in Essex stand testimony to the huge agricultural wealth of the orders. The military orders seem an anomaly today, but their large and well-farmed estates, their role in the crusades and their knightly virtues put them close to the heart of medieval life.

NUNS AND NUNNERIES

The monastic life was open to women as well as men and the first nunneries had already been set up in the Middle East during the lifetime of Pachomius. By the time monasteries were established in England under the Anglo-Saxons, some of the most inspiring and important religious figures of the period were nuns.

Abbess Hild (621–80) – also known as St Hild – was one of the most famous. She was a woman of noble birth who ran the important monastery at Whitby on the Yorkshire coast in the 7th century. Endowed by the Northumbrian king Oswy (reigned 642–70), the monastery at Whitby was originally a double house for both monks and nuns, as were several other early monasteries, including Ely, Barking and the one at Hartlepool, which Hild led before she arrived at Whitby. Whitby itself was a remarkable community. Under Hild it housed five monks who later became bishops, together with Caedmon, England's first religious poet. Hild's foundation also hosted the Synod of Whitby in 664, where the decision was made to follow the Roman rather than the Celtic church.

Anglo-Saxon history is full of high-born women who took to the cloister and some even founded their own monasteries. Queen Etheldreda, founder of Ely, and Kyneburgha and Kyneswytha, daughters of King Penda of Mercia and founders of a nunnery at Castor near Peterborough, are notable examples. Other women, such as Milburga of Wenlock Priory, became abbesses of already-established houses. Important rulers also took a hand. The most successful nunnery in the Middle Ages was the one at Shaftesbury, which was founded by King Alfred; the king's daughter, Aethelgifu, was its first abbess.

Whitby Abbey began in the Saxon period as a house for monks and nuns, but was refounded for monks after the Norman conquest. These 13th-century arches form part of the monks' church.

But in spite of these influential leaders, there were far fewer nuns than monks in the Middle Ages. Before the Norman conquest there were only around a dozen nunneries in England. By the early 14th century the number had risen to about 150, but it had fallen back to 136, housing probably about 2,000 nuns, by the time of the dissolution. There were also only a handful of nunneries in Wales.

Why were these numbers so small? Demand must have been much lower for female houses than for male. In the Middle Ages there was one clear role for women – that of wife and mother – and the vast majority of women aspired to it. From the point of view of potential founders, a male house was usually more attractive, since many of its monks would become priests, some of whom could says Masses for the founder's soul. And a male house would be more likely to grow, to the greater credit of the founder. So there were relatively few nunneries.

Most of these nunneries were small houses with an average population of fewer than 15 women. On the whole they have left scanty remains on the ground and few documents, so we know much less about them than their male counterparts. And most nunneries were not rich. Without a large male workforce they did not usually go in for the large-scale agriculture of the Cistercians – though there were exceptions, such as the nunnery of Rosedale, which had a flock of 2,000 sheep in the early 14th century. But most nunneries tended to be poorer than their male equivalents and to be modestly endowed.

The majority of nunneries belonged to the Benedictine tradition. This is true of the Anglo-Saxon foundations, such as Barking and Romsey, though we do not always know exactly which rule these early foundations

This reconstruction shows the nuns of Denny Abbey taking a meal in the 15th century while one sister gives a reading from the pulpit.

followed. Many later nunneries, from the priory of St Katherine's in Exeter to Nun Monkton in North Yorkshire, were also Benedictine. There were also a number of houses of canonesses, such as the Augustinian nunnery at Grace Dieu and the Gilbertine houses, such as that at Sempringham, which were double monasteries that accommodated both canons and nuns. This notion of double monasteries was a revival of the early tradition exemplified by Hild's Whitby. Like many reforming and renewing movements in medieval monasticism, it was in one sense an attempt to get back to the early basics.

However, many nunneries were difficult to label as belonging to a specific order or movement. A number aspired to the Cistercian way of life and set up small houses such as the Midland nunneries of Cookhill and Pinley. But the Cistercians saw themselves as a male order, so such houses were 'unofficially' Cistercian. Finally, there were nuns within the Franciscans – known as the Poor Clares after their founder – and the Dominicans. But in the Middle Ages the traditional rough-and-ready, vagrant existence of the friar was seen as unsuitable for women, so the Poor Clares and their Dominican sisters lived lives of work and prayer much like other nuns.

What we know about the nuns themselves suggests that most came from the upper classes. They could be women who had a vocation, who for some reason had not found a husband or who came to the cloister late in life as widows. Many – even those for whom the monastic life was a second-best choice – did well. They were freed from the medieval woman's usual fate of family life and home-making, and freed too from the serious health risks of childbirth in the Middle Ages. In the nunnery, by contrast, they could live long, find a different kind of fulfilment and perhaps rise to the position of prioress or abbess.

Compared to the monk, it is true, the life of the medieval nun was restricted. She could not be ordained as a priest and could not expect to wield the kind of influence enjoyed by many a medieval abbot. Nunneries – if they were not part of a double house – usually had to employ a priest to celebrate the sacraments. They might also have a male official to look after areas of land and property administration that required a man's oversight in medieval law. But in other ways the restrictions placed on the nuns opened up other opportunities for them. There was demand in many places for educated women who could teach female members of

The Second Nun, one of the pilgrims in Chaucer's poem The Canterbury Tales, *rides side-saddle in this 15th-century English manuscript.*

well-to-do families and for those who could tend women who were ill. There could be real satisfaction for the medieval nun who found her niche in such a sphere, together with the fellowship and support of a community working together to serve God.

For the nun who had a vocation for a still more focused religious life, there was sometimes the chance to become an anchoress. An anchoress's life was one of silence, prayer and seclusion, living alone in a cell but often with the support of a nearby monastery. Abbot Ailred of Rievaulx had a sister who was an anchoress and he wrote a treatise to guide her in her life apart. Some nunneries, such as Carrow and Polesworth, had anchoress's cells in their grounds, so the anchoress – though living rather like a hermit – could paradoxically be part of a monastic community too. The life of the anchoress seems to have been quite popular in the Middle Ages and one medieval text, the *Ancrene Wisse* (*Rule for Anchoresses*), survives in more than a dozen manuscripts. It was written for a number of anchoresses in the 13th century, suggesting that there were groups of women in which the lives of the cloistered nun and the hermit were in a way combined.

Brinkburn Priory was never a rich house and its relative poverty meant that there were not resources to renew many of its early buildings. As a result, many early details, like this north doorway, survived through the later Middle Ages. Buildings like this show how even poverty and decline can pay dividends for the student of monasteries.

THE MONASTERIES IN DECLINE

On the face of it, a family with a son considering the religious life, or with money to donate to a monastery, had a wide choice in the 14th century. The variety of monastic opportunities stretched from the long-established Benedictines to the isolated Carthusians, from the rural Cistercians to the urban friars. There were hundreds of monasteries and scores of friaries, and collectively they played a huge part in the life of the country.

But in practice things were not quite as rosy as these facts might suggest. For one thing, the monastic orders were no longer as different from each other as they once were. Only the Carthusians stood out in their austerity; only the friars seemed to offer a radically different approach to the religious life.

And so in the 14th and 15th centuries, the traditional life of the cloistered monk seemed less attractive to many. Abbey populations declined until by 1500 there were only 10,000 monks and 2,000 nuns in England and many monasteries numbered only a handful of brothers

or sisters. With too few personnel, it became hard for the smaller houses to manage their resources and many got deeply into debt. Meanwhile, the larger houses remained wealthy and were the cause of envy amongst the lay population.

With the decline in numbers, many abbeys had fewer resources to devote to the community. They became less important as educators. And many shirked their duty to the lay community in another way. Monasteries increasingly held powers over parish churches, collecting the tithes – the one-tenth of their produce that lay people gave to the church – in return for providing a parish priest. But abbeys often failed to provide a priest, simply sending one to celebrate Mass who would disappear after the service was over without performing any of the priest's pastoral duties. In such cases, the laity were being cheated and they did not like it.

As a result of these declining standards, all the religious orders came in for a great deal of criticism in the 14th century. The friars, who had seemed so specifically to have adopted poverty, were now lambasted, by some monks as well as by the laity, for enjoying the benefits of rich property holdings and for giving in to the temptations offered by their life amongst the laity. Others criticised the friars for their failure to perform properly their priestly or pastoral duties. Geoffrey Chaucer highlighted these perceived failings in *The Canterbury Tales*, where his friar cheats the gullible.

A 15th-century illustration of the Friar, another of Chaucer's Canterbury pilgrims.

The friars and their supporters hit back at the monks. The monks, so the argument went, were the real property owners, who enjoyed the fruits of the land, bent the rules about diet and silence, and spent time hunting, hawking or carousing with guests when they should have been serving God. There were complaints about abbots who mismanaged their estates, about monks who habitually missed attendance in church and about brothers in the company of the opposite sex.

The root of the problem was the monasteries' wealth, which led to both luxury and licence, and some argued that it should be confiscated so that the monks could return undistracted to their core activities and beliefs. Poverty, after all, was supposed to be one of the key values of monasticism. But the monks responded that their wealth had come to them because their patrons had made gifts to God. It was not for them to give back these gifts on God's behalf.

And so the arguments went back and forth. One of the most famous leaders in the debate was the teacher and religious reformer John Wyclif (1329–84). Wyclif was a priest and an Oxford-trained intellectual. He argued that all authority is founded in grace and that a wicked ruler forfeited his right to rule. Wyclif's argument applied equally to religious as to secular rulers. This was dangerous talk in a world in which leaders saw themselves as ruling with godly power. And as his career continued, Wyclif's talk became still more dangerous as he began to question the validity of the priesthood and central doctrines such as transubstantiation, the idea that the bread and wine change in substance to become the body and blood of Christ. This was too much for the church and Wyclif was eventually condemned by monks, friars and the archbishop of Canterbury alike as a heretic. But his questioning of the basis of the power of abbots and priors would not go away and others continued to probe the shortcomings of the monasteries.

The monastic community itself was shaken, but felt that it could reform itself from inside. There was, after all, a well-established system of discipline. Monasteries were visited regularly, either by the local bishop or his officials, or by a senior representative of the order. Visitors listened to complaints in confidence and acted on them, producing a report and recommendations for action. In many cases, where the problems were minor lapses and there was the will to improve, the visitor's report was probably enough to set the brothers on the right path. But in the worst cases, especially where there was a weak and lax abbot, it was hard to make the reforms stick. Visitations were supposed to be annual, but in practice it often took up to four years for the bishop or other visitor to return and abuses could multiply in his absence.

It is impossible to know, 500 years on, how bad the problem really was. Visitors' reports have survived patchily and much of the other evidence is partial, consisting of anticlerical attacks and defensive rejoinders from the victims. It is likely that many monasteries were more relaxed than they should have been, but equally likely that blatant abuses were rare. In neither case would the monks have wanted wholesale reform and, without the pressure for reform from within, the monasteries carried on largely as they were.

The group that came most under threat were the alien priories, the monasteries that had been set up under the aegis of abbeys in France.

Cluniac priories such as Wenlock, dependent on the French house of Cluny, were vulnerable during the Hundred Years War. This view shows the infirmary and prior's lodgings.

Many had very few monks and their main *raison d'être* was to manage the English estates of French monasteries. Others were larger. The Cluniac houses, for example, were effectively alien priories, because they were daughter houses of the abbey of Cluny. Large and small alike were affected when the Hundred Years War (1337–1453) saw England in continuous conflict with France. The fighting did not go on all the time, but the monasteries' fate was precarious. For the most part, they survived. Many were absorbed into larger English monasteries. The wealthier ones were able to buy a charter from the king, ending their connection with France. Their fate showed that monasteries were insecure without the backing of the king.

There is good evidence that part of the monastic establishment – the friars – enjoyed much public support in the late Middle Ages. Large numbers of laymen and women remembered the friars in their wills, apparently oblivious to jibes about their lax behaviour. Support for the friars, indeed, is probably one reason why conventional monasteries found themselves less well supported in this period. The sinking of resources into collegiate churches may be another.

But the story is not completely dismal. Many monasteries were still busy building in the 15th century, upgrading their premises or adapting them to new needs. Though some of this work consisted of providing

The church of Bath Abbey survives and is one of the best examples of the Perpendicular style, which was fashionable in the decades before the dissolution.

more luxurious abbots' quarters, it was a sign that in many places, the monasteries were confident enough and had enough money to keep investing in their buildings. One only has to look at the magnificent late Gothic architecture of Bath Abbey or the nave of the cathedral-priory at Canterbury to see that some monasteries at least were still throwing huge resources at their churches and building for the glory of God. Thus the picture in the late Middle Ages was not a simple one and, on the eve of the Reformation, monasteries varied immensely, from tiny rural houses clinging on by the skin of their teeth to vast complexes like Westminster and Glastonbury.

None of the attacks on monasticism or the attempts at reform that came in the 15th century, though, could prepare the monasteries for the broadside that they received in the 16th. For this was when they confronted their most formidable opponent: King Henry VIII (reigned 1509–47).

TOWARDS THE DISSOLUTION

By the 1530s Henry VIII's reign had reached a point of crisis. Henry
wanted to divorce his wife, Catherine of Aragon, who had failed to
produce a male heir, but this was impossible without papal approval and
the pope had not granted permission. Henry's foreign policy meanwhile
– especially his series of costly wars with France – had left his treasury
depleted.

Henry addressed the divorce crisis by breaking with Rome. Through a
series of Acts of Parliament he abolished the pope's right to jurisdiction
in England and, with the Act of Supremacy, made himself the head of the
English church. Part of this takeover of the church also helped the
financial crisis – through an Act of Parliament of 1534, the crown was
granted one-tenth of the income of the church. In order to assess how
much money Henry was due, a taxation survey called the *Valor
Ecclesiasticus* (*Ecclesiastical Valuation*) took place the following year.
Amongst other things, this gave Henry a clear account of the incomes of
all the monasteries. It made interesting reading. Some 50 per cent of the
monasteries were very small, with incomes of £200 per year or less. Only
a handful – about 4 per cent – brought in more than £1,000. The survey
also established that of all this money, only about 3 per cent was spent on
works that benefited the lay community.

*The dissolution was not the only
death knell for the monasteries.
Creake Abbey was a small
Augustinian foundation that closed
in 1506, after most of the canons
had succumbed to the plague.*

As head of the English church, one of Henry's duties was to oversee the monasteries. He in effect took over the role of Visitor of the abbeys and priories, and the Act of Supremacy gave him the power 'to visit, repress, redress, reform, order, correct, restrain and amend all such errors, heresies, abuses, offences, contempts and enormities …which ought or may be lawfully reformed'. To this end, Henry appointed his minister Thomas Cromwell to the role of Vicar-General, with the responsibility of sending out agents to inspect the religious houses.

The royal Visitors were laymen who acted swiftly and critically. The wording of the Act of Supremacy gave them every indication of what they were expected to find and their swift inspection – they did not visit every monastery – brought many abuses and offences to light. They found pregnant nuns at Lichfield, an abbot benefiting from the profits of piracy at Whitby and monks drunk at Mass at Pershore. The once-great abbey at Battle was condemned as 'beggary' and 'filthy stuff', while the famous phial of Holy Blood at Hailes, which had been the goal of pilgrims for almost 300 years, was condemned as a concoction of honey and saffron.

The reports of the Visitors gave Henry the ammunition he needed. He could close the monasteries on a wholesale scale, at the same time wiping out what looked like global abuse and corruption while getting his hands on substantial property. Land, buildings, gold and silver plate, bells, lead from roofs, books and countless furniture and chattels – there were rich pickings to be had from the monasteries.

The legal machinery to appropriate this property was soon in motion. Henry began with the smaller monasteries. It was an interesting decision, since there was no correlation between moral standards and income. But they were less powerful and presumably easier to cow. In 1536 an Act was passed closing the 50 per cent of religious houses that had been valued at £200 or less together with any others with fewer than 12 monks or nuns. The Act presented itself as a moral edict, condemning the laxity of the smaller houses and praising the larger monasteries as places where religion was properly observed. But the most significant clause was the one that gave Henry the right to the property of the dissolved houses, which the king 'should have and enjoy'. The dissolution was under way in earnest and there was no doubt about who would be the main beneficiary.

A monk with greyhounds is illustrated in this manuscript of The Canterbury Tales, *which was produced in the 15th century when monks were often accused of corruption and inappropriate activities.*

In many cases, the monks and nuns suffered little. Most were either transferred to another house of their order, pensioned off or allowed to become parish priests. Some 70 of the targeted monasteries were allowed to escape dissolution by buying exemption. But these facts conceal a more sinister truth. Many abbots and monks agreed to the dissolution under duress, signing confessions of misdeeds that certainly would not have stood up in a modern court of law.

In the north, there was some resistance. Conservative Catholics did not like what the king was doing – and they also had social and economic grievances – and rebellions broke out. The trouble started in Lincolnshire in October 1536 and spread northwards under the leadership of Yorkshire gentleman and lawyer Robert Aske. He assembled some 35,000 followers, seized the city of York and began to march south. His banner depicted the five wounds of Christ and the movement he led became known as the Pilgrimage of Grace.

Thomas Howard, Duke of Norfolk – the leader of the king's forces – met Aske at Doncaster and made a deal for peace. Norfolk – with the king's backing – agreed to address the rebels' grievances and the rebellion broke up. But Henry had no intention of submitting to the rebels' demands, which included dismissing Thomas Cromwell and restoring papal jurisdiction. Further outbreaks of trouble in Yorkshire in early 1537 – some of which Aske himself tried to quash – gave Henry excuse enough to come down hard. The rebellions were suppressed, Aske was executed and a number of 'treasonable' Yorkshire abbots were also hanged.

The Pilgrimage of Grace was a local rebellion. Few people in the south stood up against the dissolution of the monasteries and this fact alone must have encouraged Henry to widen the net. In 1537 and 1538 Cromwell carried on probing the monasteries in a further wave of suppressions, putting pressure on vulnerable houses to agree to closure. There was every incentive to cave in – monks and nuns who went quietly were more likely to come out of the process with the prospect of a comfortable life.

And so, whether by coercion or bowing to the inevitable, abbot after abbot signed surrender deeds, handed over the keys of his abbey to Cromwell's commissioners and watched as the incomers made a detailed list of the abbey's possessions. It would have been a painful business, standing by while centuries of tradition disappeared in an action which most must have seen as despicable and impious.

There was compensation for those who went without complaint. At Roche Abbey, for example, each monk was allotted a pension, the amount depending on the individual's position in the abbey. The abbot, as a person of the highest rank, was paid off more handsomely. Abbot Henry of Roche had his pension topped up with an extra £30, a quarter of the plate belonging to the abbey, books, household goods, a chalice and a certain amount of corn. An abbot who was recompensed in this way must have felt bought off – Henry was keeping possible objectors and rebels quiet, and almost giving them a vested interest in the dissolution.

Many abbots collected their benefits and eventually got powerful and rewarding jobs in the church. There were a number of former abbots amongst the bishops and higher clergy of the Tudor cathedrals. Those who wanted a quiet life retired with enough income to live out their lives as country gentlemen. Lower down the hierarchy, numerous monks became parish priests or returned to life outside the church. There were no such employment options for the nuns, many of whom married.

Shrines and relics were condemned by opponents of the monasteries. This reconstruction shows the shrine at Rievaulx.

The year 1538 also saw the dismantling of monastic shrines, many of which yielded rich booty in the form of items made of precious metals and encrusted with jewels. Then the friars were disbanded. Since their property was held in trust for them anyway, they had little bargaining power and won no pensions. Most were left to live by their wits. This left the last of the larger houses, which were all dissolved by the early months of 1540. The great Benedictine abbey of Evesham and the famous Augustinian house at Waltham were the last to go down.

The financial benefit to Henry was vast. The monasteries had held enormous amounts of land, all of which now passed to the king. But Henry's situation was difficult. His treasury was virtually bankrupt and he needed cash quickly, so much of the monastic land and possessions were sold on at low prices to willing buyers. Charles Brandon, Duke of Suffolk, snapped up the property of some 30 monasteries. Many other aristocrats made similar gains, often selling on some of their newly acquired property to others further down the social scale. There was thus a certain redistribution of wealth around the country, though this should not be exaggerated. Most of the beneficiaries were already landed. Henry was not creating a new landed class – but he was ensuring that there were plenty of lay people who gained from the dissolution and would support him.

The result of the dissolution was felt immediately on the church's buildings. Most monastic churches were deliberately turned into roofless ruins so that they would not attract anyone attempting to start a monastic revival. Stripping valuable lead from the roof, taking the glass from the windows and removing some of the better stone for recycling was a way of turning a profit and putting a church beyond use. Abandoned churches became quarries. They were crown property, or the property of those who bought them from the king, and their stone was there to be exploited. Some would have been sold off, some pilfered by opportunist locals who could wait until the owner's back was turned. Today many English towns and villages have Tudor or Stuart houses with fragments of medieval masonry built into them here and there, the fruits of bargaining or theft. Such plundered material was especially attractive in areas – such as East Anglia – where good building stone was scarce. And so, as stones were removed, the sad but evocative monastic ruins that are still such a feature of today's landscape came into being.

In the towns things were slightly different. Space inside town and city walls was at a premium and few buildings were simply left to become ruins. For example the buildings of the friars were usually quickly converted for secular use. Many have subsequently been demolished and replaced, so friary remains are scarce.

Bayham Abbey's ruins were left to decay after the dissolution and eventually became a picturesque feature in an 18th-century landscaped park.

Over the years a variety of buildings have 'colonised' the medieval abbey walls at Bury St Edmunds.

In some places the local parish was able to secure part of the church for the use of the lay population. Inspiring and informative fragments of great monastic churches survive in many places, from the Cistercian Dore Abbey to the Benedictine Croyland, where the parish still uses the north aisle of the church next to the ruined Gothic nave. Elsewhere, entire monastic churches survive in use, like the large Benedictine church at Tewkesbury, where the parishioners claimed the nave as their own and bought the monastic east end for £453.

The great cathedral-priories have also survived. The fate of Norwich, the first of them to be dissolved, was typical. The church was re-established as a secular cathedral, manned by a dean and chapter instead of a prior and monks. The last prior was appointed dean and a number of the monks found positions in the chapter, while others became parish priests in the diocese. As for the servants and officers of the priory, some were pensioned off and others were likely to have been kept on in their posts. The church survived as Norwich Cathedral, but the other buildings underwent change. The fine cloister survived, with its stunning series of carved roof bosses, but most of the rooms to which it gave access – including the chapter house, refectory and guest hall – were demolished. The infirmary beyond also became a ruin. But the prior's lodging survived: it became the deanery, which it remains.

There were also new bishoprics based at some of the former abbeys. The abbeys of Bristol, Chester, Gloucester, Oxford and Peterborough became cathedrals. As a result their churches and some of their other buildings have been preserved, structures which, in the case of Gloucester and Peterborough at least, are now recognised as having international importance. Therefore the dissolution of the monasteries, in most ways so destructive, left behind a few buildings that are still admired, enjoyed and used today.

Norwich's cloister survived the dissolution and its roof bosses are some of the finest in medieval architecture. This roof boss depicts the sealing of a tomb.

Medieval monasteries

A MEDIEVAL ABBEY WAS NOT SO MUCH A BUILDING as a group of buildings of different shapes and sizes clustered together and walled off from the rest of the world inside a closed precinct. These buildings ranged from vast edifices the size of cathedrals to tiny structures hardly larger than a garden shed. For the most part, they are now ruins, with walls a few metres, or only a few centimetres, in height. All of this makes them rather baffling to the modern visitor.

A medieval monk or nun, by contrast, would have had little such difficulty, because most monasteries were laid out to a standard pattern and each building or room was designed so that it suited exactly the activities that went on inside. That is not to say that every monastery was designed in exactly the same way – there were some variations between the monastic orders and adjustments were sometimes made to suit specific building sites. But on the whole, a monk from England who had to travel to France would instantly be able to find his way around when he visited other houses of his order and, for the most part, monasteries belonging to other orders too.

This chapter looks at the different buildings of the monastic precinct in turn, examining both what went on in them and how they were designed. It examines the cloister – the rectangular space with its four walks, off which most of the main domestic accommodation of the monks or nuns could be found; it looks beyond the cloister at the other, usually free-standing, buildings dotted around the precinct; and it describes the way the precinct was protected by walls and gatehouses. Finally, it takes a look outside the walls to consider some of the monastic buildings beyond the precinct and some of the ways in which abbeys influenced the medieval countryside and townscape. But it begins at the heart of the monastery, with the most important building of all: the church.

The east end of Rievaulx Abbey, one of the most evocative of all medieval monastic ruins.

THE MONASTIC CHURCH

The principal purpose of the life of the monk or nun was the communal worship of God. The inhabitants of a monastery could spend as much as half their waking lives in church and so the church was the largest and usually the most beautiful building in a monastery. Religious communities poured resources into their churches and even a small monastery could have a large church. The reason for this is that a church was not simply a utilitarian building, planned to accommodate a specific number of worshippers. The building of a medieval church was itself an act of worship, dedicated to the glory of God. Therefore church builders in the Middle Ages usually tried to put up the most magnificent building they could afford. Typically, when a new monastery was founded, the community would initially make do with wooden domestic buildings and the church would be the first structure to be built in stone.

When the monasteries were dissolved by Henry VIII, the churches were often the first buildings to disappear or to be left to decay. Abbey churches are still some of our most evocative ruins. But some churches

A view of Lanercost Priory shows the typical cruciform layout of the monastic church. Here the four 'arms' are arranged around a central tower.

did survive in whole or in part, to be used as cathedrals or parish churches. Both the ruins and these survivors have much to tell us about the monastic way of life and worship, and about the kind of architecture favoured by the different religious orders.

The huge part of the monastic day taken up by the liturgy can be appreciated by looking at the timetable observed by a monk or nun. This varied according to the time of year (the day began earlier and finished later in summer, when there was more light) and there were also differences between orders and historical periods. But the basic framework remained constant, structured as it was around the eight canonical hours of the divine office.

A typical monastic day in the 11th century might begin at 2.30am when the monks awoke and prepared for the night office, known as nocturns, which was sung at 3.00am. After returning to the dormitory the community would rise again at 5.00am and read for an hour until the next office, matins, which took place at daybreak and was followed by the third office, prime. More reading was followed by the fourth office, terce, at around 8.00am, and the first Mass of the day, the morrow Mass. The next event in the monastic day was chapter, the monastery's daily meeting dealing with business and discipline. By 9.45am chapter would be over and the community would begin their first stint of work before the fifth office, sext, at midday. Sext was followed by Mass and at 1.30pm by the sixth office, none, before the house took its main meal at around 2.00pm. At 2.45pm came the second session of work, lasting until vespers, the seventh office, at 4.15pm. Collation (a reading on the monastic life) at around 6.00pm was followed by the final office, compline, and bed at about 6.30pm.

The offices were based on the singing of psalms. There were also prayers, both for the souls of the departed and for the living, especially the benefactors of the abbey. In addition on saints' days and other important religious festivals – especially at Easter – there would be additional services and rituals. Further observances were introduced at various points during the Middle Ages. A daily Mass of the Virgin was celebrated from the 12th century. Periods of private prayer were introduced in some orders before nocturns, before terce and after compline. Masses for the dead were said in some periods. And so on.

There were also variations between the ways the different orders performed their observances. The Cluniacs in particular developed an elaborate liturgy, with processions and rich vestments on major feast days. These elaborations were also taken up in other monasteries, though the Cistercians rejected them, seeking to bring back the importance of work in the monastic timetable and cutting down on the elaborations – for example they banned bells and costly vestments. The Augustinians were also known for shorter services. The friars followed the hours but, as enthusiastic preachers, emphasised the importance of compline because, coming as it did at the end of the working day, it was the only service that could attract a sizeable lay congregation. The Carthusians sung only matins, vespers and Mass in church; they said the other offices on their own in their cells.

So the orders followed a broadly similar liturgical programme and monastic churches on the whole evolved in a similar way to accommodate this. Anglo-Saxon monastic churches varied greatly. Most have disappeared, replaced by later buildings, so evidence has to be gathered from archaeological excavation and study of the fabric of those that survive as mostly much-altered parish churches. Some were quite simple, almost barn-like buildings, though archaeology reveals that a major monastery such as Jarrow or St Augustine's in Canterbury could

The church at Deerhurst is one of the best preserved early monastic buildings. The tower and many of the walls are Saxon, although most of the windows were inserted later in the Middle Ages.

have two or more churches, built end-to-end. Other monasteries, such as Deerhurst, where the church survives in parochial use, had complex churches with various side rooms – known as porticus – plus other chambers and galleries, each of which no doubt had a specific religious purpose, from housing singers to displaying relics. By the time of the Norman conquest, however, a more standard kind of monastic church plan was evolving.

Most post-conquest monastic churches have a cruciform or cross-shaped plan, oriented east–west. In the eastern arm of the cross is the choir (or quire) where the monks or nuns sang the hours with the guidance of the precentor, the abbey's director of music. East of the choir is the presbytery, the area that housed the high altar. The northern and southern arms of the church – the transepts – provided space for additional altars so that monks who were also ordained priests could say their own daily Mass. This leaves the western arm of the church, the nave. In many monasteries this was reserved for any lay people –

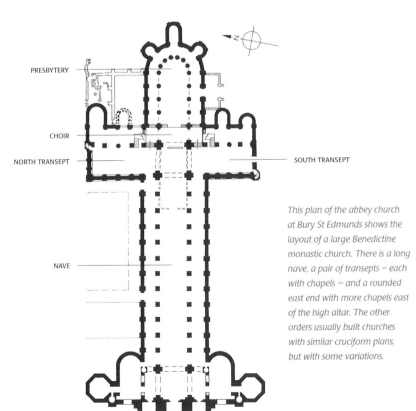

PRESBYTERY

CHOIR

NORTH TRANSEPT

SOUTH TRANSEPT

NAVE

This plan of the abbey church at Bury St Edmunds shows the layout of a large Benedictine monastic church. There is a long nave, a pair of transepts – each with chapels – and a rounded east end with more chapels east of the high altar. The other orders usually built churches with similar cruciform plans, but with some variations.

especially the abbey's guests – who might come to one of the services. Sometimes the nave or one of its aisles was specifically reserved for lay use – it acted as the local parish church. In Cistercian monasteries the main purpose of the nave was to accommodate the lay brothers, who attended services but did not sing the hours with the choir monks.

The main entrance to the church was usually at the west end; larger churches often had an elaborate west front with one or more doorways, above which were niches containing statues and several large windows. This entrance was open to the laity and was the public face of the church; on a large building such as a major monastery or cathedral-priory it could be a stunning piece of architecture. The monks or nuns, though, had other entrances into the church, which linked it to their domestic accommodation. Usually there were two doorways leading into the cloister, allowing the monks or nuns to process into church through one doorway and out through another – the Cistercians, who used a different processional route, sometimes did without one of these doorways. In addition, there was a night stair, which linked the dormitory (*see* pp 110–12) directly with one of the transepts, so that there was a suitable direct route into the church for the night office.

Visitors to a large medieval abbey church would enter through one of the west doors and would find themselves straight away in the nave, which was the lay portion of the church. This was a grand, even awesome, space. Tall and long, it was flanked by rows of arches separating the nave from its aisles. Above these arches were still more, smaller, arches, forming a gallery called the triforium and above these was a row of windows, called the clerestory, which threw light into the nave. In the grandest churches, the whole space was topped with a stone-vaulted ceiling. But even many large abbey churches had a wooden nave roof with no vault, because vaults were costly and presented huge engineering challenges; the nave was the biggest space in the church so here a vault would be expensive indeed.

The nave was separated from the choir by a substantial screen called the pulpitum. The pulpitum could take various forms from an elaborate stone screen adorned with figures of saints or kings to a more lowly wooden structure. But the pulpitum always had the function of dividing the choir from the western portion of the church while also allowing access through a central door. The screen was nowhere near as high as

Even with most of its great window bricked in, the Gothic west front of Binham Priory is still elegant and beautifully proportioned.

Above the large arches of the nave arcade and the smaller openings of the triforium, tall clerestory windows let light into the church at Brinkburn Priory.

A reconstruction of the church at Rievaulx in the mid-13th century shows the choir monks in their stalls.

the building, so there was a space above it through which lay worshippers in the nave could glimpse the choir and hear the choir monks singing the office.

The choir itself (with the presbytery beyond) was designed in a similar way to the nave, with arches, a gallery, a clerestory and sometimes a vaulted ceiling. It was furnished with wooden stalls, set in two ranks facing each other across the middle of the space. Choir stalls could be remarkable works of carpentry, with carved canopies in the Gothic style. Also remarkable were the seats, known as misericords, which tipped up to form a support for choir members who had to stand for long periods. The undersides of these seats, visible when they were tipped up, were often adorned with amusing carvings of a mixture of subjects, from beast fables to grotesques; these can still be found in some of the monastic churches that have remained in use.

The grandest churches had a passage, called the ambulatory, running either side of the choir and presbytery and around the east end. This gave access to chapels arranged around the east end of the church and could also form a route for pilgrims visiting the church's holy relics.

Though the cruciform plan was widespread, there were variations in layout according to the beliefs and requirements of the different orders. Because the Cistercians believed that churches should be relatively austere and unadorned, they often favoured square east ends in contrast to the curvaceous apses favoured by other orders. They also generally did without the tall towers seen on many monastic churches. But these are not hard-and-fast rules. There were some Cistercian churches with apses (such as Hailes) and with tall towers (Fountains). In a similar way, the Augustinians often built churches with unaisled naves, but there were notable exceptions.

The Cluniacs had many monks who were priests, so their churches contained numerous spaces for altars where Mass could be said. Nuns, by contrast, could not be priests, so nunneries did not need a profusion of altars. The friars were preachers and liked to build churches that were like large halls – they were not divided up with screens in the way that Benedictine or Cistercian churches were. Instead of a pulpitum, a friary church usually had an area, known as the walking space, between the nave (which was often aisleless) and the choir. However, the most distinctive of all monastic church plans were those of the Knights Templar. The Knights built round churches, in imitation of the Church of the Holy Sepulchre in Jerusalem – the Temple Church in London is a good example that still stands. Its nave has a central circular space surrounded by arches, with clerestory windows above them flooding the building with light.

Other changes in architecture took place across the orders as a result of alterations in liturgical fashion. For example the liturgy of the Mass became more elaborate after the Fourth Lateran Council in 1215. This council of the church formulated a new definition of the Mass, in which the notion of transubstantiation was central. The view that the bread and wine become the body and blood of Christ during the Mass, coupled with the more elaborate ritual that went with it, is probably the reason behind the 13th-century fashion for building longer and more complex east ends – a development that affected secular as well as monastic churches. Another development – increased reverence for the Virgin Mary and the custom of celebrating a daily Mass in her name – gave rise to the building of countless Lady Chapels, usually right at the east end of the church, beyond the high altar.

Because the monastic history of the medieval period stretched from the Saxon era until the dissolution under Henry VIII, churches could be built in a variety of different architectural styles. Often there were different styles in the same building, since major medieval churches were big building projects that took decades – at least – to complete and were frequently expanded and modified when benefactions allowed. An abbey church could have a Norman nave built in the decades after the conquest, a Gothic choir from the 13th century and chapels in the late Gothic style built on the eve of the dissolution. It helps our appreciation of these buildings to know something of how these different styles varied and how fashions in church architecture changed through the centuries.

Though a few Saxon abbey churches survive in part, they have been much altered. Therefore our first clear view of monastic architecture is from the profusion of buildings put up by the Normans. Norman buildings usually have thick walls and the arches – both in nave arcades and atop doorways and windows – are semicircular. Their window openings are simple in design and are not subdivided by stone bars to produce the tracery often seen in later windows. And in many Norman buildings, the ornament is also simple, with geometric patterns, such as the chevron, or simple mouldings adorning their arches.

Thus Norman abbeys can look plain but impressive in their size and grandeur, with rows of round-headed arches lining the interiors of churches such as Binham and Romsey. Some of the most imposing are the Norman naves of the Benedictine churches of western England, such as Gloucester, Tewkesbury and Leominster, in which the structures are held up with gigantic plain round piers. But Norman architecture can also be more ornate. At the cathedral-priory of Durham, the piers are decorated with incised geometric decoration in zigzags, cross-banding and fluting, and the patterns are carved in extra-large size, so that they are in proportion with the enormous building. This kind of carved decoration on big piers is rare, but it is also found at Selby and Waltham.

Blind arcading, a common form of ornament, is often found on Norman outside walls. This takes the form of a series of blank arches just proud of the wall surface, sometimes in two 'layers' so that they overlap. It is a form of decoration that looks good on the west front of a church as

At Ely, the prior's doorway is topped by a superb Norman relief of Christ in Majesty flanked by angels.

it catches the light, especially when combined with round-headed windows and doorways with a number of recessed arches. This sort of effect is seen on a number of Cluniac buildings, including the priories at Castle Acre and Much Wenlock, and the ornate surface it produces seems in keeping with the Cluniac love of elaborate ritual and rich vestments. But this type of decoration is not exclusive to the Cluniacs. The Augustinians also favoured it at the priories at Colchester, Christchurch and Bolton. And blind arcading of great beauty has survived on some Benedictine churches. The magnificent tower at Tewkesbury, probably the best surviving Norman church tower, is a good example.

All this decoration is abstract, showing the Normans' talent for pattern-making, but there were also figurative carvers of genius amongst the Norman masons. The cathedral-priory of Rochester has a fine Norman doorway, this time on the west front, with a carved semicircular panel, or tympanum, above. Doorways are indeed the best place to look for Norman carved reliefs and one of the best is at Malmesbury, a Benedictine church with a south porch of remarkable sculptural power. Abstract and foliage patterns scroll their way around the doorway in several bands, enclosing a semicircular tympanum above the door that depicts Christ flanked by

angels. The east and west interior walls of the porch are still more
stunning. They bear lunette-shaped reliefs in which groups of six apostles
sit, with angels flying above them. The deeply-carved drapery with its
linear folds, the faces, the poses – some with heads bent as if meditating,
some all attention – mark these carvings as masterpieces.

Most of the abbeys that contain extensive Norman work belonged to the
Benedictine, Cluniac or Augustinian orders. Soon after the reforming
orders established themselves in the 12th century, a new style of church
architecture was sweeping Europe: Gothic, a type of architecture based on
the pointed arch. It was developed – mainly in France and especially at the
abbey of St Denis near Paris – to allow larger windows so that churches
could be flooded with light and become three-dimensional metaphors of
God's presence. Gothic builders reduced the amount of wall between the
windows until the stonework almost disappeared between the panels of
stained glass. This meant that supporting the heavy stone-vaulted roofs
was a challenge, a challenge they met with flying buttresses that bridged
the roofs of the aisles, taking the weight and strain towards the ground.
Thus pointed arches, large windows, thinner walls, flying buttresses and
high stone vaults are the hallmarks of Gothic buildings.

Gothic architecture was dynamic. It kept developing throughout the
Middle Ages. In the 19th century, architectural historians developed a
way of talking about English Gothic architecture as if it consisted of
three main phases, which they called Early English, Decorated and
Perpendicular and which were fashionable in the 13th, 14th and 15th
centuries respectively. These labels are useful, but they do not define
precise periods; medieval masons did not think in terms of rigid styles.

Nevertheless, the earliest English Gothic buildings did share features
in common. Narrow, pointed windows, known as lancets, replaced the
round-topped openings of the Normans. The pointed arches were deeply
moulded and often flanked by miniature columns called shafts. Piers
could also be surrounded by shafts. And vaults were pointed and divided
by ribs, thin bands of stone that provided a sort of structural skeleton that
held the ceiling together. One of the most beautiful examples of this style
is the Augustinian priory at Hexham, where the church was built in
around 1200 and is full of tall, elegant lancet windows, some flanked
with bundles of slender shafts. Another is the east end of Dore Abbey,
a remote Cistercian building on the border with Wales, which is now the

*The dormitory range at Cleeve Abbey
has pointed Gothic windows with
simple tracery.*

local parish church. Here lancets, shafts and ribbed vaulting combine beautifully together. This austere but elegant way of building found particular favour with the Cistercians, whose order was growing when it was fashionable. Their great Yorkshire abbeys of Rievaulx and Fountains have early Gothic east ends. This early pointed style survives in many other places, including smaller churches such as Boxgrove and larger ones such as Whitby, both belonging to Benedictine monasteries. The 13th century was a time of much church-building, especially of more elaborate east ends.

In many early Gothic buildings, lancet windows are used in groups and soon masons were finding ways of combining several lancets in a single complex window, with three or more glazed sections, or lights, topped with tracery. Building in this way gave masons the chance to dispense with even more stone walling and fill their churches with more

Elaborate Gothic tracery of the early 14th century fills this huge window at Dorchester Abbey in Oxfordshire.

light. Thus in the late 13th and 14th centuries, windows were developed
further and a whole vocabulary of tracery evolved. In the hands of some
builders this elaborate tracery was combined with richer decorative
carving, to create the style the Victorians called Decorated.

At its most florid, the Decorated style of Gothic architecture displays
rich carving, complex and curvaceous window tracery, a multitude of
pinnacles often adorned with more carving and a liking for the ogee –
a double curve first convex then concave – in doorways and windows.
It is a rich style, creating an effect somewhat at odds with monastic
austerity, and thus it is not a style much associated with the Cistercians,
whose great building boom in any case took place in the late 12th and
13th centuries.

However, there are some Benedictine abbeys with outstanding
Decorated Gothic details. For example the east end of Selby Abbey's
church was rebuilt in the Decorated style. There is a large east window
with the most curvaceous tracery, and a host of pinnacles, some topping
buttresses, others acting as roofs to little octagonal turrets, and all studded
with crockets, carved decorations popular with 14th-century builders.
Inside there are forests of shafts each surmounted with a capital that is
carved in the classic Decorated manner, many with naturalistic foliage.

An Augustianian house – Dorchester in Oxfordshire – inserted some
stunning windows in the 14th century. In the choir, these have tracery
that, unusually, fills the entire window, not just the top. And this tracery
is not made up of plain bars of stone but is richly carved. In one window,
carved figures perch amongst the uprights while the curving tracery bars
form branches and foliage. It represents a Jesse Tree, a visual
representation of the lineage of Christ, beginning with Jesse, the father of
David.

The same theme is depicted in another Decorated masterpiece, the
reredos (the decorative panel behind the altar) at the Augustinian church
of Christchurch Priory. Many of the figures have disappeared from this
reredos, but the remaining carving of the Adoration of the Magi, with two
Magi in conversation while one kneels before Jesus and Mary, shows the
quality of the work.

Sculpture like this shows how medieval artists and monks could pour
their devotion into art while also using that art to tell the story of their
faith. This was also something they did with stained-glass windows,

*The reredos at Christchurch Priory
is not the only carved decoration.
More modest examples include this
carved corbel.*

though these were too luxurious and colourful for the most austere
Cistercians. Cistercian abbeys were not supposed to have stained glass
and a number of reprimands came from the mother house to abbeys
where the monks – and no doubt their lay benefactors – could not
resist them. Those benefactors were also commemorated in beautiful
14th-century carving. Tomb canopies, like those of the members of the
Dispenser family who supported the Benedictine house at Tewkesbury,
are amongst the glories of the Decorated style.

The 14th century brought a final revolution in medieval church
architecture – the rejection of the curvaceous Decorated style for the
Perpendicular, an architecture based largely on straight lines. This style
was unique to England and began at court in the 14th century before
becoming popular in church architecture in the 15th. The earliest abbey
structure in this new idiom was the choir of the building that is now
Gloucester Cathedral. This vast space was remodelled after the death of
Edward II in 1327 to house his tomb and it sums up Perpendicular
architecture. At the east end there is no wall at all, just one vast window
divided by upright stone mullions and horizontal transoms into a series
of panels, each perfectly proportioned to accommodate a single stained-
glass figure. This panelled effect is continued on the flanking walls, but
here the lower levels of panelling are blind – only the upper level has
clerestory windows to let in light from above. The whole space is capped
with a ceiling vaulted with an intricate web of intersecting ribs. At each
meeting point of these vaulting ribs is a large carved stone called a boss –
some depict angels, others flowers or foliage – giving the whole ceiling a
feeling of richness. Though the Perpendicular framework is quite plain
(it is basically a grid of uprights and horizontals), the Gloucester choir
typifies the way in which the details, especially the stained glass and roof
bosses, could be quite lavish.

The style of the Gloucester choir spread throughout England during
the 15th century. Hundreds of parish churches were rebuilt in the
Perpendicular style – those in East Anglia and Somerset are particularly
outstanding. But by this time the monasteries were in decline. The
numbers of monks and nuns were falling, anticlericalism was rife and
lay patrons were pouring their funds into other branches of the church –
for example into their parish churches or into collegiate churches.
Nevertheless, there does seem to have been a brief revival in monastic

*One of the earliest structures in the
late medieval Perpendicular style,
the choir at Gloucester is dominated
by the enormous east window.*

building not long before the dissolution and many abbeys have some detail or other – perhaps a gatehouse, an aisle or a walk of the cloister – in the Perpendicular style.

Amongst abbey churches there are one or two with fan-vaulted roofs, their upturned cones of ribs one of the last great achievements of English medieval architecture. Fan vaults appeared first at Gloucester, where they roof the narrow spaces of the cloister walks. Sherborne Abbey has fan vaults on a much larger scale in the nave and the abbey at Bath has the best collection of fan vaults of all – nave, crossing, choir and aisles are all vaulted in this way. The whole is a design of the first two decades of the 16th century, though the great nave vault was not actually built until the 19th century. It is the swansong of English medieval architecture.

Bath Abbey is unusual in that it is one virtually coherent design. Most medieval churches grew organically, leaving behind work from several different periods. No doubt there were two reasons for this hybrid quality of medieval churches. Cost alone must have prevented many complete rebuildings. But the fabric of previous periods often had a sacred quality and there must have been something positive about retaining work from earlier ages. It is a quality that we can still recognise today both in the monastic churches that survive in use and in the tantalising ruins, some still standing almost to ceiling height, that have stood since the monasteries were closed by Henry VIII.

The ornate west front of Bath Abbey was completed only a few years before the dissolution.

SHRINES AND RELICS

Sacred relics played an important part in medieval life and monasteries were their custodians. The ranks of the saints are extensive. They range from Biblical figures known throughout Christendom to those with a local connection, such as St Milburga, the first abbess at Wenlock Priory, or fathers of the Anglo-Saxon Church, such as St Aethelwold, bishop of Winchester. After they had died, the bodies of such figures were revered and enclosed in shrines that were set up in prominent places in churches. Other holy relics, such as pieces of the True Cross, were also kept and venerated.

Examples such as Milburga and Aethelwold indicate that saints and relics were important from the Saxon period onwards. Edith, who rebuilt the nunnery at Wilton just before the Norman conquest, was following in a long tradition when she took pains to find relics for her monastery. A number of fine monastic crypts survive from just before and just after the conquest and these may well have housed important relics and the tombs of saints. The cathedrals at Worcester and Gloucester, both originally important Benedictine churches, have beautiful early crypts, with plain pillars, rounded arches and vaulted ceilings.

These early crypts seem to speak of the remote and simple piety – more distant even than the relic cults of the Gothic period – of the saints who were the founding parents of British monasticism. Such saints continued to command the respect and reverence of the Normans (*see* p 28) and the people of the later Middle Ages. For example the remains of the Anglo-Saxon saint Cuthbert continued to be venerated at Durham. St Albans was still honoured as the resting place of Alban, the 3rd-century Christian who became England's first martyr. St Etheldreda, 7th-century founding abbess at Ely, was still revered in the 13th century, when the east end of her church was rebuilt to make a better setting for her shrine. St Swithun, Winchester's 9th-century saint, continued to be venerated in the later Middle Ages. And many abbeys collected relics from a number of saints, ancient and more recent.

In the later Middle Ages, pilgrims were still flocking to the shrines. Chaucer's *The Canterbury Tales*, written in the late 14th century and the most famous English medieval poem, describes a group of pilgrims on their way to the resting place of St Thomas Becket at Canterbury, one of

Winifred, a Welsh saint, is commemorated on a carving at the entrance to the chapter house at Haughmond Abbey, in the border county of Shropshire.

the most popular of all English shrines. Major centres like this were often said to be the sites of notable miracles. So the sick went on pilgrimage to be cured, while others undertook the journey to affirm their faith.

The presence of pilgrims must have transformed the atmosphere of a medieval abbey church. The travellers came from all over Britain and, in the case of major centres, even sometimes from continental Europe. In many places it was customary for them to spend a night in the church, praying or sleeping near the shrine. One or more of the monks or nuns who acted as wardens of the shrine had to join the pilgrims to police this activity, for parties of pilgrims might well include those whose behaviour was not up to standard. At major pilgrimage centres there were nearly always some visitors and the numbers increased at major festivals and saints' days. Pilgrimage made work for the inhabitants of a monastery, but it also brought dividends in the form of gifts, benefactions and income for the abbey's inns. Pilgrimage, in other words, was a major part of the monastic economy.

This was especially the case for a major monastery such as Canterbury. St Thomas Becket (1118–70) was a popular and famous saint, renowned as a churchman who had stood up for his beliefs and been killed by the henchmen of Henry II as a result. Soon after his martyrdom, the monks of the cathedral-priory at Canterbury set about remodelling the east end of their church to house his shrine. But if a monastery lacked its own resident saint, relics could be collected from elsewhere and brought back to the monastic church. The treasures of Reading Abbey, for example, included relics of St Bernard of Clairvaux and other foreign saints such as St Bridget and St Philip, as well as items purporting to be the swaddling clothes of Jesus and the belt of the Virgin Mary. Such items brought visitors and offerings to an abbey and gave benefactors the chance of a burial place amongst the relics in a sacred space and an atmosphere of reverence.

Many monastic houses collected such relics and many of these items sound as spurious to modern ears as those proudly kept at Reading. Mottisfont preserved the finger of St John the Baptist. Canterbury possessed clay said to be some of the clay that God used to make Adam. Fragments of the True Cross were scattered all over Europe and if they had been brought together they would have made many crosses. But medieval people wanted to believe in relics, so many accepted their authenticity without question. However, people also knew that false relics were common. The Fourth Lateran Council, presided over by Pope Innocent III in 1215, condemned false relics and those who traded in holy remains. Newly discovered relics had to be approved by the pope himself. And churchmen were admonished not to fool pilgrims into giving alms when they visited relics that were known to be false.

This anxiety was understandable. It was in a monastery's interests to possess powerful relics and to become a fashionable pilgrimage centre. A famous case was the Cistercian abbey at Hailes. Hailes was founded in 1246 by Richard, Earl of Cornwall (1209–72), probably the richest man in England after the king. To begin with, the abbey did not do well. The house ran up debts in order to pay for building work and for a time the monks seem to have stopped giving alms to the poor, presumably to save money. But in 1270 the fortunes of Hailes were transformed when Richard's second son, Edmund, gave the monastery a phial that was said to contain some of Christ's blood. Edmund had bought the relic and it came with a guarantee of authenticity from the Patriarch of Jerusalem,

This artist's impression shows the famous shrine of the Holy Blood at Hailes at the east end of the abbey church, as it might have been in the 14th century.

the man who later became Pope Urban IV. Once installed in a special shrine in the abbey, the blood turned Hailes into a goal for pilgrims. Visitors flocked to the shrine and, once the monks had recovered from the cost of more building work to house the relic and the pilgrims, the abbey prospered. The success of Hailes lasted until the dissolution, when it was revealed that the blood was not genuine.

Not surprisingly, other monasteries wanted the special blend of spiritual and worldly benefits brought by sacred relics and countless abbey churches contained shrines. Other famous pilgrimage centres, in addition to Canterbury, were Glastonbury (said to have been visited by Joseph of Arimathea and also the resting place of St Dunstan and many other saints), Broomholm (keeper of the Holy Rood, a small cross made from wood alleged to be from the True Cross), Shaftesbury (housing the shrine to Edward the Martyr) and Walsingham (where there was a copy of the house of the Virgin Mary supposedly made at her command). Slightly less popular but still well known were the shrines at Durham (St Cuthbert), Lincoln (St Hugh), Ripon (St Wilfrid), Whitby (St Hild), Winchester (St Swithun) and so on. Wales also had pilgrimage centres. Bardsey was well known as the burial place of numerous saints, while Strata Florida, itself on the route between St David's and Bardsey, displayed an ancient cup that was supposed to be the Holy Grail.

At the dissolution, this reverence of relics was brought to an end. Shrines were broken up and many of the relics were destroyed. Because of this, there are scant remains of England's medieval shrines. Sometimes there is tantalising evidence in a document of the magnificence of these structures. For example a canopy of silver and gold was made for the shrine of St Edmund at Bury in the late 12th or early 13th century. And surviving reliquaries – the containers in which the actual relics were housed – are often masterpieces of medieval metalwork, jewellery and enamelling. The world of medieval shrines was a lost one of bright colours and glittering metals.

The few shrines that do remain survive only in part. One of the best is that of England's first martyr at St Albans. It is a 14th-century structure, mainly made of Purbeck marble, richly carved in the Decorated style of the time with elaborate arches and foliage. At one end is a relief panel showing Alban's martyrdom, at the other a similar panel showing his scourging. Other figures on the shrine may be Offa, king of Mercia, and

St Oswyn, an Anglo-Saxon king who had been killed standing up for justice and had thus been made a saint. Oswyn's relics were at Tynemouth, a cell of St Albans, hence the connection. Another shrine, that of St Edburg from the abbey at Bicester, survives in the parish church at Stanton Harcourt in Oxfordshire – it was moved here by the local lord at the dissolution. Again it has a superstructure of Purbeck marble with statues and carved heads and miniature vaulting inside.

The shrines of St Alban and St Edburg, fragmentary and damaged as they are, show something of the richness and importance of these medieval structures. We can also glimpse this significance through the remains of the architecture that housed the shrines. Many monasteries embarked on a building campaign when they acquired an important relic. The reasons for this were twofold. First, the spiritual reason: a sacred relic deserved a fitting home, so the best architecture that the abbey could afford was erected to house it. Second, the practical consideration: the pilgrims that the relic attracted also needed space.

Shrines were usually placed at the east end of the church, so this was often remodelled. A shrine ideally needed a space separate from the area used by the monks for their services, so that the canonical hours could be observed without interruptions from the continuous traffic of pilgrims. Therefore a special chapel or space would be built for the shrine. The round chapel known as the Corona, built for Becket's shrine, survives at Canterbury.

Many east ends were remodelled to make a passage behind the high altar, with a series of chapels radiating from it. Pilgrims visiting the shrine could then move around the passage in an orderly line, entering at one end and leaving at the other. This arrangement is known as a chevet and it was the design chosen by the monks at Hailes when they acquired the Holy Blood. Many other monastic churches were given chevets, which provided the twin advantages of a processional route and a number of chapels that could either house shrines or altars where monks could say Mass.

A complex east end with an ambulatory passage and chapels had been a feature of many English greater churches for some time. It was especially common in western England, where it was used in great Benedictine abbeys such as Worcester, Great Malvern, Gloucester and Tewkesbury. Such buildings may in turn have been influenced by the

design of French pilgrimage churches, such as Mont St Michel.

Another way to develop the church's east end was to create an extension at right angles to the main east–west axis of the building. Such a space formed the Chapel of the Nine Altars at Fountains Abbey and there was a similar chapel at Durham, home to the relics of St Cuthbert. Once more, the relics were given their own special place and were kept away from the monks, whose regular worship was not to be disturbed more than necessary.

The world of the medieval pilgrim, with its hopes of miraculous cures and its atmosphere of adventure in a time when travel was slow and difficult, seems remote in a secular age. Yet thousands still visit Lourdes and Compostela, and Walsingham remains a popular destination for pilgrims in England. The scene met by pilgrims who arrive at these places, with its strange mixture of reverence and commercialism, is probably closer to that in a medieval pilgrimage town than we might imagine.

At Hailes today only the foundations of the east end remain and a low mound marks the site of the shrine of the Holy Blood.

THE CLOISTER

The cloister is the rectangular courtyard surrounded by four covered walks connecting the main domestic accommodation of a monastery to the church. In the middle of the cloister was an open area called the garth, which was usually laid to grass but sometimes also contained a fountain or a herb garden; in a Carthusian monastery this area was used as a burial ground. The cloister was a special and beautiful structure that was used in a variety of ways, so walking in a cloister brings us close to the heart of the life of the medieval monk or nun.

The cloister was usually built to the south of the nave, though there could be other arrangements to suit a particular site – at Buildwas, for example, the cloister is to the north of the nave, while at Rochester it is to the south of the chancel. Where the usual arrangement was followed, the northern cloister walk adjoined the nave. The other three cloister walks contained doorways leading to the main monastic apartments – including the chapter house, parlour, dormitory, refectory and, in Cistercian houses, the lay brothers' accommodation. The cloister was therefore central to a medieval monastery, so central indeed that its name has actually become a synonym for a religious house – we talk about 'entering the cloister' or a 'cloistered life'.

In the 13th century the cloister at Kirkham Priory had an ornate washing place, as shown in this reconstruction.

As well as acting as corridors, the cloister walks were also used to house various activities. The walk nearest the church was generally the study area and could be equipped with carrels, the small bays in which monks and nuns sat to read or write (*see* pp 101–4). The western walk often acted as a schoolroom for the novices. In addition, the alleys of the cloister were places where the inhabitants of the monastery could walk, meditate and pray.

If the cloister was at heart a practical structure, medieval cloisters are also often amongst the most stunningly beautiful parts of the monastery to which they belong. A typical cloister has stone-vaulted walks with rows of arches looking into the central garth. These arches were originally

The fine 15th-century cloister at Lacock survived the dissolution and the conversion of the abbey into a private house.

open to the elements but were often later glazed or provided with wooden shutters or leather curtains to keep out the draughts.

The first monasteries did not have cloisters. Archaeological work on early sites such as Jarrow has revealed a cluster of domestic buildings and workshops around one or more churches, with gardens and a cemetery adjacent. But by the 9th century, cloisters were becoming common in continental Europe and documentary evidence for an ideal cloistered monastery exists in the form of a manuscript plan from St Gall in Switzerland. The cloistered plan became common in Europe when it was widely adopted by the Cluniacs and it was taken up extensively in England after the reforms of St Dunstan in the mid-10th century.

The first cloister in England was at Glastonbury, Dunstan's monastery, and there were two late Saxon cloisters at St Augustine's Abbey in Canterbury. But ancient cloisters such as these exist only as fragmentary remains that have been excavated and reconstructed by archaeologists. Rebuildings and refoundations have meant that more substantial remains of cloisters date from after the Norman conquest.

It is only in the post-conquest cloisters that one can get an idea of the character of the architecture; however, even here the evidence is thin on the ground. At Rievaulx, for example, some of the shafts and arches of the Norman cloisters have been found and reconstructed on site. Pairs of shafts (and a quartet of shafts at the corner) support very plain, 12th-century arches. The architecture is typical of the Cistercians, who valued austerity and avoided architectural ornament, at least in their early days.

In the later Middle Ages cloisters were sometimes more lavishly decorated, with lots of carvings of Biblical subjects. They could also be more complex spatially. A few cloisters, for example, had an upper floor to provide extra space for study or books. Both Evesham and St Albans had this arrangement and there is a fragment of a two-storey cloister at the small monastery at Muchelney, so this was not exclusively a feature of the larger abbeys.

Some of the most outstanding later medieval cloisters are preserved in the English cathedrals. A number of these were cathedral-priories in the Middle Ages or became cathedrals shortly after the dissolution; their continuing role as cathedrals has meant that many of their monastic buildings have been well preserved. The cloister at Norwich, for example, was rebuilt over a long period from 1297 to around 1430. The overall

One corner of the cloister, with its round-headed Norman arches and slender shafts, has been rebuilt at Rievaulx.

In many abbeys a grand doorway, like this fine Norman one at Lilleshall Abbey, connects the cloister with the church.

layout is uniform, but the passing generations of masons varied the design of the tracery in the openings. But the glory of this cloister is its vaulted ceilings, which contain almost 400 stone bosses at the intersections of the vaulting ribs, all of them beautifully carved. Scenes from the lives of Christ and the Virgin appear, as do bosses representing the Apocalypse. There are also some showing scenes from the life of St Thomas Becket.

Worcester is another of the cathedral-priories with a notable cloister of the 14th and 15th centuries. Again there are many bosses, with those above the southern walk standing out; subjects include scenes from the life of the Virgin. Many medieval vaulted roofs are so high that the carvings of the bosses are hard to make out. But a cloister roof is much lower and the bosses can be appreciated in all their glory, a magnificent gallery of medieval sculpture that would have provided the monks with many subjects for prayer or meditation.

A third outstanding cloister, this time in a cathedral that started life as an abbey, is at Gloucester. Here the cloister has no carved bosses – it is the architecture rather than the sculpture that impresses. This is in the Perpendicular style, which was new in the 14th century when the cloister

The cloister at Gloucester is delicately fan-vaulted. Two of the monks' study carrels can be seen to the left.

was constructed. The fan vaults, slender shafts and stone wall decoration that looks like window tracery show the masons at the height of their power.

Thus a cloister was much more than a series of corridors. Cloisters were amongst the most arresting examples of medieval architecture and there is nothing like them in later buildings. Scenes of study and meditation, they were both practical and beautiful.

THE SCRIPTORIUM

After regular participation in the liturgy, the next most important activity of a medieval monk or nun was work – and the rule specified manual work, work with the hands. For most people in the Middle Ages, manual work meant toiling in the fields, growing the crops and raising the animals that provided their food. Monasteries also had to produce food, of course, but servants were often hired for this work, leaving the monks or nuns free for another kind of labour – study.

Unlike most of the medieval population, choir monks and nuns were literate. Many of them worked every day reading, writing and, above all, copying books because, before the invention of printing with movable type, every text had to be written out by hand. On the face of it, this does not sound like manual labour. But the monk who was writing was using his hands in the laborious task of transcribing texts accurately and – usually – beautifully. The manuscripts produced often combined the flair of the artist with the labour of the artisan.

This type of work began early in the history of monasticism. Some of the first missionaries, like the Irish St Columba, were notable scribes. And Bede, author of the *Ecclesiastical History of the English People* is one of the first great writers of English literature. Countless anonymous monks carried on the work of composition and transcription, swelling the monastic libraries until the dissolution.

The monks and nuns knew that this was vital work. Monasteries needed books if they were to pursue scholarship and the friars, with their preaching ministry, saw books as vital tools in their work of explaining the faith to others and guiding them away from heresy. It was a cause for celebration when a monastic recruit from a well-to-do family brought with him a collection of books as a gift to his new monastery or when a wealthy patron donated volumes from his library. But for the most part, if nuns or monks needed books, they had to be copied, perhaps from volumes loaned from another monastic house. To copy such texts was God's work – as St Bernard said, 'Every word you write is a blow that smites the devil.'

All the monastic orders took part in this important work. The friars were notable scholars. So too were the Carthusians, who lived a contemplative life in their solitary cells, a life that was especially suited to study and the copying of manuscripts. But the other orders contributed their share, increasing their stock of manuscripts, sending them to brother and sister houses and to monasteries of the other orders and even sometimes working for lay patrons.

What kinds of books were copied in the monasteries? The most pressing need was for the service books used every day for the divine office and for readings in the refectory. There were a number of different volumes. Missals contained the words and directions for celebration of Mass. Lectionaries were collections of extracts from the Bible to be read on specific days in the church year. Antiphoners were books of sacred chants. Psalters were collections of psalms, the singing of which was at the heart of the office. Breviaries were books containing words and music for the divine office. There were also books explaining the liturgy and scriptural commentaries used in Bible study. And the monks would want to supplement their monastic library so some scribes might be engaged in copying lives of the saints (often used for readings as well as for reference), the writings of the church fathers or works of church history. Perhaps surprisingly, even secular works – from science to poetry – were copied in monastic scriptoria.

Monasteries also played an educational role in which books were needed. As well as educating their own oblates and novices, early monasteries, especially in the Anglo-Saxon period, also provided schooling for some outsiders. Text books, such as Latin grammars, would be required for this work. As time went by, and the custom of taking oblates into monasteries declined, it also became less common for outside children to be schooled in a monastery, though there were monastic schools set up outside the precinct and staffed by lay teachers. But novices always needed instruction and books were necessary for this.

This ornately illuminated page is from a missal, dating from around 1430, one of the books acquired by St Augustine's Abbey in the 16th century.

Those with special artistic talents worked on the decorations for which medieval books are now so well known. Title pages and the opening words of chapters were decorated with appropriate illustrations that complemented and blended with the text. This decoration was done in a spirit of worship, to produce the most beautiful texts to celebrate the glory of God. The vignettes such manuscripts provide – especially those that portray everyday medieval life – are still a source of delight and information to historians.

Some monks were able authors and the creation of new books was encouraged in the cloister. Much medieval literature was written in monasteries and it included works of grammar, history and mathematics, as well as books of devotion and religious commentary. The monasteries were centres of culture where, at various times and in various places, writers, artists and composers were nurtured.

Standards of scholarship varied, but they could be very high indeed. Men often came to the monastery after a career outside it and this career could include a long involvement in the world of letters. For example Thomas of Marlborough, who was abbot of Evesham between 1229 and 1236, had studied in Paris under Stephen Langton and had a career teaching law at Exeter and Oxford at one time. Many others had been schoolmasters or had done the rounds of universities from Bologna to Oxford. There was a close relationship between the friars and the universities of Oxford and Cambridge from the 13th century onwards. The Benedictines had a house of study at Oxford by the late 13th century. And even the Cistercians, renowned for keeping a distance from the world and even from towns and cities, sent many monks to the universities in this period.

The Luttrell Psalter, *dating to around 1325–35, is one of the finest medieval English manuscripts, prized for its charming scenes of everyday life such as this one of a woman feeding chickens.*

The scholarly activity of a monastery took place in a part of the complex called the scriptorium. This could be a dedicated room but was often one of the cloister walks, commonly the northern one, next to the south wall of the church. Visitors to English medieval abbeys will find nothing of the wooden reading desks at which the monks or nuns sat as they transcribed or wrote their texts. But a few traces remain of their presence. For example some cloister walks still contain carrels, the spaces where monks and nuns studied. The cathedral (formerly the abbey) at Gloucester has a set of 20 carrels beneath the windows of one cloister walk – they have survived because their structure is of stone and is fully

This reconstruction shows the monks of Rievaulx Abbey at work at their wooden desks.

integrated with the Perpendicular architecture of the cloister. Carrels are also preserved at Durham and there are traces of them at other sites such as Beaulieu. However, because they were made of wood, most of them have vanished.

The work that took place in these carrels was painstaking and slow. Copying a full-length book was a project that could take months or even years and the parchment for a complete Old Testament could cost an entire flock of sheep their skins. Thus many monastic libraries began as quite small collections. Glastonbury Abbey, for example, was for much of the Middle Ages the richest monastery in England and also one of the largest. In 1247 its library consisted of around 400 volumes. Another major monastery, Canterbury Cathedral Priory, had around 1,850 books in the 13th century and the total rose to something like 4,000 at the dissolution. Clearly this was one of the great medieval libraries and about 300 of its books have been identified as still surviving today. Durham, Worcester, Bury St Edmunds and St Augustine's in Canterbury also had substantial libraries.

Though these collections have been dispersed, evidence of their storage remains. It is provided in some monasteries by the presence of book cupboards built in the form of stone alcoves in the cloister walls.

Carrels line the first-floor southern range of buildings at Gloucester Blackfriars. Each carrel has a window, to provide light for reading and writing.

The alcoves in the cloister at Hailes, for example, were probably cupboards that housed the monastery's library. Such alcoves would originally have had wooden shelves and doors – and probably wooden linings to keep out any damp that might seep through the porous stone cloister walls.

Some Cistercian abbeys also had a dedicated storeroom – accessed from the cloister and adjoining the north transept – which may have been used for books. At Fountains the vestibule of the chapter house had two areas that were walled off and probably used for this purpose. At Cleeve the library was in a small, barrel-vaulted room north of the chapter house. It had a single small barred window and a lockable door, for the contents of any medieval library – in which each volume was the fruit of long labour – were highly valuable.

Cluniac priories usually had book cupboards or libraries on the eastern range of the cloister near the south transept of the church. A good example of a library survives at Wenlock Priory. It is a long, narrow room with a floor covered in fine medieval tiles. There are now three entrances, though two of these were made after the dissolution, when the building was used as a farm.

In the later Middle Ages, as monastic book collections increased in size, more and more dedicated libraries were provided – for example the libraries at Bury St Edmunds and Norwich were on an upper floor of the cloister, at Worcester in a room above the south aisle. These are meagre

Wall niches, which would originally have had wooden doors and shelves, were used for book storage at Lilleshall Abbey.

remains, but these plain rooms and simple spaces are where, with the most basic equipment and materials – parchment, quills, inkwell and ruler – monks and nuns put together some of the greatest works of medieval art.

THE CHAPTER HOUSE

Every day the monks or nuns held a meeting to discuss discipline and the daily business of the monastery. This meeting took place after morning Mass and was known as chapter, because a chapter of the rule was read before discussions began. It was held in a special room called the chapter house and, like the canonical hours, it was one of the fixed points in the monastic day.

Before the meeting formally began, the members of the monastery would walk to the chapter house and take their seats around the walls. The head of the monastery would preside – or, in his or her absence, a deputy such as the prior or prioress – and would take a seat against

The monks of Hailes have assembled for chapter in this reconstruction. The chapter house doorway and cloister can be seen in the background.

the east wall; the obedientiaries would sit on either side of their abbot or abbess. The meeting would begin with the reading of an extract from the rule and perhaps also with a lesson and an address from the abbot.

The business proper then began and generally this was of two kinds. First, chapter gave the opportunity for the brothers or sisters to confess their faults. They might own up voluntarily to any breaches of the rule they had committed or they might be accused by their colleagues. Either way, the abbot would assign a penance, in the same way that a secular priest would do in the more private setting of the confessional. There is evidence that some monks found this process intimidating, trembling as they hoped not to be accused of a fault and silently wishing for a light penance. Much would have depended on the head of the monastery and how he or she ran the meeting and meted out the penances.

Then there was the day-to-day business of the monastery to be discussed. Obedientiaries might need to ask for extra help in their tasks; there might be reports of work on outlying farms or granges; there could be discussions of plans for coming fairs or religious festivals; sometimes there would be business or tenancy agreements to sign and witness; and so on. A monastery was in some ways like a medieval corporation and chapter could resemble both a board meeting and a managerial briefing.

Chapter, then, was one of the main focuses of the day for the inhabitants of a monastery. Decisions made there could affect the life of a monk or nun for days, weeks or perhaps even for years. In keeping with its importance, the chapter house was often the most impressive space in the monastery after the church. It would not be as large as the refectory with its tables or the dormitory with its beds, but its architecture could be magnificent. Fortunately, a number of monastic chapter houses have survived, both in cathedrals that began life as monasteries and at some of the ruined sites, and these give an idea of the setting of these daily meetings.

The chapter house was usually a large room on the eastern range of the cloister near to the church. In many monasteries it was a ground-floor room with part of the dormitory, the main upper-floor room on the eastern range, above it. This arrangement meant that monks or nuns in the dormitory had easy access to the church for the night office. But in many larger monasteries, the chapter house was a double-height room between dormitory and church. To permit access to the church for the night office, therefore, double-height chapter houses were often approached from the cloister by way of a lower vestibule, over which was a passage that ran between the dormitory and the church.

The earliest surviving chapter houses are Norman and are amongst the most ornate surviving Norman rooms. Bristol Cathedral, which was originally an abbey of the Augustinians, has one of the best, dating to around 1150–70. Seats for the canons line the walls, each topped with a simple round-headed stone canopy. Above are rows of quite ornate interlaced arches, enriched with cable and other ornate mouldings. Higher still the stone walls are carved with lattice and zigzag patterns. The whole is topped with a stone vault, its ribs adorned with deep zigzag carving. It is a high-status room of breathtaking beauty. Other Norman chapter houses, though ruined like that at the Cluniac Wenlock Priory, show similar high-quality masonry. Many, such as those at Haughmond and Furness, have a magnificent entrance doorway framed with recessed orders of arches and flanked with smaller but similar openings on either side.

These stunning rooms must have been amongst the most lavish of any in the early Middle Ages. They provided a fitting setting in which abbots transacted business, dispensed discipline and, sometimes, received important visitors. When an abbot of the 12th or 13th century died, he was usually buried not in the church but beneath the floor of the chapter

Haughmond Abbey still has its grand chapter house doorway, flanked by a pair of windows under sweeping arches.

At Westminster Abbey, the high vaulted ceiling of the chapter house is supported on a single slender central column.

house, so that his successors seemed to speak with the combined authority of all the previous abbots of the house.

Most of these early chapter houses were rectangular, though some were made church-like by apsidal ends. But there was a fashion slightly later in the Middle Ages for polygonal chapter houses, spaces that provided an almost circular meeting room. One of the earliest was at the cathedral-priory of Worcester, which is indeed almost circular and has Norman arcading with later Gothic-style windows above.

But the most influential building was the great chapter house at Westminster Abbey, a stunning, tall octagonal space built by Henry III in the 13th century and heavily restored in the 19th. Its features – wall seats topped with Gothic arches, huge windows, a soaring vaulted ceiling supported by a central column and lavish carving – were imitated in many later chapter houses. Some of the best preserved examples can be seen in the great cathedrals, but there are also remains of polygonal chapter houses at monasteries such as Bolton, Pontefract and Thornton. They were amongst England's great medieval rooms and stand as fitting testimony to the importance of the discussions that once took place beneath their elegant vaulted ceilings.

THE PARLOUR AND WARMING HOUSE

Monasteries were supposed to be silent places, where the calm was broken only by the chanting of the office, readings during meals and the discussions of chapter. Restrained conversation must have been necessary as monks or nuns went about their business, but silence was the aim and some orders even used sign language to communicate and avoid making noise. One part of the monastery in which the rule of silence was relaxed was the parlour. This was a small room off the cloister where conversation was allowed for limited periods of time. The parlour was usually on the eastern range of the cloister, near the church, and often next to and parallel with the slype, a connecting passage linking the cloister with the part of the precinct to the east that often contained the monastic cemetery and the infirmary. Parlours in this position can be found at many monastic sites, including Castle Acre, Fountains, Rievaulx and Roche.

The parlour was typically a narrow vaulted room with stone benches along opposite walls. Most surviving monastic parlours, such as the one at Thornton Abbey, do not look especially inviting places – they were probably kept fairly spartan in order not to offer too much temptation for monks or nuns to linger and talk longer than was necessary.

There was sometimes a second parlour, in or near the western cloister range, which was provided for meetings between the inhabitants of the monastery and visitors. This room could be in a number of different

The parlour at Buildwas is a small, rather austere vaulted room.

locations and was sometimes, as at Castle Acre, adjacent to the lodgings of the head of the monastery. It could be quite a grand room, as was fitting for receiving visitors.

Another room that gave monks or nuns some respite and comfort was the warming house, which was originally the only place in a monastery apart from the kitchen and the infirmary where a fire was allowed to be lit. The warming house, which sometimes also doubled as the parlour, was usually close to or beneath the dormitory. This meant that its fire also brought some warmth to the monks or nuns when they were in their beds.

The warming house was prized in the early Middle Ages, especially by those who were engaged in work in the cloister or scriptorium. Sedentary scribes got cold quickly and a session in the warming house was vital from time to time. But as monasteries generally became more comfortable in the later Middle Ages, with more fireplaces – and probably fewer draughts – the heating role of the warming house became less significant and it came to be seen as a parlour pure and simple, and a more desirable one than the old, early-medieval parlours with their inhospitable stone benches.

Enough of the fireplace survives in Byland's warming house to show its size and to give the impression that the room might have been both warm and comfortable.

THE DORMITORY

Most monks or nuns slept in a large communal room called the
dormitory (also known as the dorter), which was usually on the upper
floor of the eastern range of the cloister. It was a long room, usually
with a row of windows along each side. The early medieval conception of
a dormitory was a room laid out rather like a hospital ward – the beds
were arranged in rows without any partitions in between. The only other
furniture would have been wooden chests or lockers for clothing. There
was no privacy, though this was not unusual as many of the laity in the
Middle Ages also had to do without privacy, with many members of the
same family sleeping in a single room.

However, by the 14th century, things were changing. Privacy was more
highly valued and dormitories began to be divided with wooden partitions
so that they resembled a series of small cells. This was in spite of a
number of prohibitions against dividing up such rooms. Each unit would
contain a desk and seat as well as a bed, so that the monk or nun could
read and write as well as sleep here. In many cases, each person had his
or her own window to provide natural light for reading – such windows
can still be seen in the room now used as the library at Durham
Cathedral. The individual compartments of the dormitory had become
like small private study rooms, quiet zones that were perhaps more
conducive to study and meditation than the small carrels in the cloister
walk where many monks studied.

Partitioned into cells, the late medieval dormitory would have looked
comfortable. But dormitories were unheated and were never luxurious
places. The best the inhabitants could hope for was that the wooden
partitions would give them some protection from the draught and that a
little heat would rise from the fire in the warming house, which was
usually beneath the dormitory.

More important than heat in the monastic scheme of things was
access to the church. Monks and nuns had to rise for the night office so
there was usually a communicating door and stair between the
dormitory and the nearby transept of the church. By using this night stair
they could be out of the dormitory and in their places in the choir in a
few minutes. Few night stairs remain – either because monastic
buildings are now often ruins or because surviving churches have been

given over to parish use. But one survives at the Augustinian priory church at Hexham.

One of the best-preserved dormitories is at Cleeve Abbey – it is a long mid-13th-century room, typical in that it began life as one large space that was later divided by partitions. The partitions have long since disappeared and the room is a single space again. It is lit by rows of lancet windows that were originally fitted with wooden shutters. Doorways lead to the night stairs and to the reredorter (the building that housed the latrine), while a set of day stairs leads down to the cloister walk to give access to all the monastery's main domestic rooms. Today the bare stone is visible in most of the interior walls, but areas of ancient limewash contain a masonry pattern in red – a typical medieval pattern that would originally have been repeated all over the walls. These fragments have remained thanks to the protection of the room's timber-framed roof, which was renewed in the 17th or 18th century.

At Cleeve, the dormitory survives with its roof. It is a long upper-storey room with windows looking on to the cloister garth. The day stairs are in the foreground.

Few dormitories have survived roofed and protected as Cleeve's has done. The one at Forde is roofed, but now makes up part of a later country house and has been altered and converted into smaller rooms. But a number of monastic dormitories remain as roofless shells, their walls long and high enough to reveal what magnificent rooms they once were – Battle, Castle Acre and the extraordinarily long dormitory at

A view from the south-east shows the row of windows that lit the dormitory at Jervaulx.

Furness are good examples. And the plans of many dormitories can also be traced from the evidence of the rooms on the ground floor below, including a number of vaulted undercrofts and warming houses that are interesting medieval rooms in their own right. Battle Abbey has one of the best of these undercrofts, with ribbed vaulting held up on simple, circular piers. Battle was founded in 1067 by William the Conqueror, in thanks for his victory in 1066 and as a place where prayers could be said for the souls of those who fell in the conflict. The dormitory undercroft at Battle is actually a later structure, of about 1200, but it is appropriately grand for a royal abbey. However, many such rooms were smaller, lower and altogether less impressive.

THE REFECTORY

The communal monastic dining room was known as the refectory (or frater). In winter, one meal a day was taken here, at around 2pm. During the longer days of summer there were generally two communal meals, at midday and about 5.30pm. Just before mealtimes, the inhabitants of the monastery processed to the refectory, which was usually on the side of the cloister furthest from the church, pausing at the nearby washing place or laver (*see* pp 121–2) before entering and taking their usual seats. There was a high table for the head of the monastery (unless he or she ate in their own lodgings), tables for the monks or nuns and a separate table for the novices. After grace, all ate in silence, while one of their number went to the raised pulpit that was a prominent feature of the room and read from the Bible or one of the lives of the saints, for Benedict wanted them to be hungry for spiritual as well as bodily sustenance.

The food they ate was meant to be frugal but sufficient. Meat was not generally allowed and most meals consisted of bread, vegetables, cheese and cereal. Extra dishes, known as pittances, were permitted on special occasions and could consist of eggs or fish. This was the theory and in many monasteries for much of the time the letter of the rule was no doubt followed. But there were exceptions – for example those who were ill were allowed to eat meat, and abbots, who frequently had to entertain important guests, often had a more lavish table than their charges.

BELOW LEFT:
The imposing refectory at Rievaulx was lit by tall lancet windows. Since the floor has long gone, the basement can also be seen.

BELOW RIGHT:
The refectory at Beaulieu was converted to a parish church after the dissolution. The stone pulpit, where a monk read while his brothers ate, was preserved.

The rule could be stretched further. At various times the Benedictines, Cluniacs and Augustinian canons were all criticised for eating forbidden foods (especially meat) or for eating too much. Therefore reforming orders such as the Cistercians placed a heavy stress on the correct diet, banning luxuries such as eggs during Lent and Advent, prescribing the coarsest black bread and generally enforcing the letter of the rule.

The Carthusians, too, were strict about diet. Inhabitants of the charterhouse normally prepared their own meals in their cells using the ingredients provided each day. Three days a week the monks survived on bread and water and on other days the diet was spartan and meat-free. Only on Sundays and feast days did the Carthusian brothers sit down together in the refectory and even then the food was usually frugal.

But few orders were as zealous as the Carthusians or the Cistercians in their first flush of reforming enthusiasm. In many monasteries, meat-eating continued and sometimes monks took turns to eat in a second dining room where meat or richer food was served. Many monks also looked forward to spending time in the infirmary, where richer food was also on offer (*see* pp 129–30). In some places the fare was on a par with what was available in a rich manor house. In the first half of the 15th century, menus at the prior's table at Durham, for example, included salmon, oysters and dates. Though most of the time the ordinary monks enjoyed simpler fare, they were invited in turn to the prior's table, so all got a taste of these riches, as well as the chance to wash their food down with wine rather than the beer that was on offer in many monasteries.

The refectory where these meals were endured or enjoyed was one of the largest rooms in the monastery. It usually occupied all or almost all of one range of the cloister with its long sides parallel to the cloister walk and it was often built above an undercroft that was used for storage. In Cistercian houses, where the cloister had to provide separate facilities (including a second refectory) for the lay brothers, the choir monks' refectory was usually built at right angles to its usual position with its short ends parallel to the cloister walks, so that other rooms could also be accommodated on its side of the cloister. When the custom of admitting lay brothers disappeared, some Cistercian houses went back to the more traditional layout of cloister and refectory.

Either way, a monastic refectory was a long room with a wooden roof, a pulpit for readings and a devotional image such as a crucifix or Christ

The refectory undercroft at Finchale Priory has a fine ribbed vault of around 1320.

in Majesty on the end wall. There could be wall alcoves near the door, perhaps for storing cutlery and napkins, and a hatch to the adjoining kitchen, through which the food was served. Quiet and clean, it could be an impressive room, as surviving examples testify.

At many sites of ruined monasteries the refectory has virtually disappeared. But its size and position can often be traced from the remains of the undercroft beneath and these storage rooms are themselves often impressive structures. At Lanercost Priory, for example, there is a vaulted undercroft of the mid-13th century. It was divided into two rooms in the Middle Ages – six of the vaulted bays were used for storing food and drink and the three western bays had a fireplace and were used as the canons' warming room. Finchale, another northern priory, also has a fine undercroft, dating this time to the early 14th century, and here part of the walls of the refectory itself, with rows of tall lancet windows, survives above.

At Fountains Abbey the refectory walls are still mostly at full height, revealing several of the room's key features. There is a finely moulded entrance doorway and the six lancet windows on each side can still be seen, as can the position of the pulpit in the west wall. Evidence for the position of the tables and the plinth of one of the columns that supported the roof of this 110 × 40ft (33.5 × 12m) room also remain.

Cleeve Abbey's refectory range has an impressive row of 15th-century windows.

But perhaps a smaller abbey like Cleeve, a Cistercian establishment, provides an even better impression of the atmosphere of a medieval refectory. Here the refectory was rebuilt in the 15th century after the disappearance of the lay brothers, so it is positioned in the traditional way along the length of the southern cloister wall. It is a light room, with rows of tall windows and a dais at one end for the high table. Though a number of important features, such as the pulpit, have been removed and the painting of the Crucifixion on the end wall has faded away, the magnificent medieval timber roof remains, resting on angel corbels. This superb piece of carpentry is adorned with further angels and bosses bearing carved foliage. There are also fine refectories at Denny Abbey (with a superb 14th-century tiled floor), Durham (later converted into a library) and Worcester (where a large statue of Christ in Majesty provides a striking devotional focus). Such rooms, with their fine window tracery and religious paintings or sculptures, act as good reminders of the way the orders sought spiritual nourishment as they ate.

THE KITCHEN AND FOOD STORES

Abbeys usually aimed to be self-sufficient in food. Most houses held extensive lands and, though some of these were commonly let to tenants, some were farmed directly by the monastery and could be tended either by the monks or by abbey servants to provide food for the inhabitants. Since meat-eating was forbidden, officially at least, much monastic agriculture was devoted mainly to cultivating crops and dairy farming. Crops included wheat and rye to make flour for bread; various vegetables and pulses (such as peas, cabbages, onions and leeks); and barley for brewing. Milk and eggs were also produced. And abbey precincts also often contained a herb garden to supply both culinary herbs and ingredients for the medicines used in the infirmary.

The organisation of monastic agriculture and the storage of its produce was the realm of one of the most important of all the obedientiaries, the cellarer (often called a cellaress in a nunnery). The cellarer was not just responsible for the cellars and other storage rooms in the abbey – it was also his job to appoint those who looked after the abbey's farms and to oversee abbey servants. He was a busy man, even with the assistance of his sub-cellarer and often had leave of absence to visit the abbey's farms and granges or to go to fairs and markets. He thus became a key link between the closed world of the precinct and the outside world. When he was at home, the cellarer worked in his own office, or checker, where he kept his accounts and planned the logistics of the abbey's supplies. This office was often a small room conveniently near to both the cellar and the kitchen.

The cellarer worked hand-in-hand with the kitchener and, from his store rooms, the produce went to the kitchen and bakehouse, where it was made into the plain fare usually eaten by monks and nuns – coarse bread, vegetable pottage or soup and other simple dishes. Barley would go to the brewhouse where it was made into beer.

The kitchens were usually the least showy of monastic buildings. They were often tucked away, detached from the main cloister range and conveniently close to the refectory and the water supply. They could also be located at the end of the western cloister range furthest from the church, again close to the refectory. In a Cistercian monastery, where the kitchen had to serve separate dining rooms for the choir monks and lay brothers, it was found between these two refectories.

Nowadays ruined monastic kitchens can be identified by the fireplaces they contain. In monasteries there were usually few fires outside the infirmary and warming house, but a kitchen could contain more than one. A large abbey could have several kitchens – as well as the main

The vaulting of the cellarium is glimpsed through a window at Waverley Abbey.

A pair of large fireplaces marks the site of the canons' kitchen at Haughmond Abbey.

kitchen there might be one for the abbot and another serving the
infirmary. These are nearly all in ruins now; to imagine such kitchens at
work, one must conjure up in the mind's eye a battery of equipment and
a number of cooks and servants wielding it. There would be several
cauldrons for cooking pulses, vegetables and pottages, and for heating
water for washing up; several large sink-like containers for washing
vegetables and kitchen vessels; a number of knives and a sharpening
stone; spoons, large and small; urns, strainers and pots; protective
clothing such as gloves and sleeves to slip over the habit; and containers
for herbs and seasonings.

The kitchener presided over all this equipment and over the frantic
activity that often erupted around it – especially when the abbey was
playing host to lots of guests for a special occasion such as a feast day.
He would be helped by a number of cooks – there was a tradition that
the monks or nuns took turns to work in the kitchen, but as time went
on there were more and more specialists, including, in large abbeys, a
number of paid kitchen servants. And in houses where the rule was
observed less strictly, with richer foods and meat allowed, the work could
be demanding and complex.

*The buttery was a storeroom for
food and drink. The one at Netley
has an arched hatch so that supplies
can be passed through.*

With its octagonal stone roof and ornate lantern, the 14th-century abbot's kitchen at Glastonbury was one of the finest service buildings of the Middle Ages.

Only one monastic kitchen survives more or less intact and this is the abbot's kitchen at Glastonbury. Glastonbury was a major Benedictine abbey with probably the longest history of any English monastery. Its line of abbots included St Dunstan, the prime mover of the English monastic revival of the 10th century. By the 14th century, though, abbots were living a more comfortable life than Dunstan would have recognised, with a much more varied diet than the regime of pottage and vegetables that many monks and nuns had to face. The abbot of Glastonbury built a magnificent kitchen to supply his table. The kitchen is square in plan, but ranges are built across each corner to create an octagonal room inside. The roof also is eight-sided, tapering to an octagonal lantern that forms a louver through which smoke from the ranges could escape. Elegant two-light Gothic windows illuminate the interior.

The Glastonbury abbot's kitchen is unusually grand. It served a large abbey where the church alone, at 550ft (168m) in length, rivalled England's longest cathedral at Winchester. But the abbot's kitchen is not quite unique since there is a similar square, octagonal-roofed kitchen at the manor house at Stanton Harcourt in Oxfordshire. The abbot's kitchen, though, is the more sophisticated design. At Stanton Harcourt there are no chimneys – smoke had to find its way out through the roof. But at Glastonbury a system of flues took the smoke from the ranges to the lantern at the top. Like so much medieval architecture, the building is technologically clever as well as impressive to look at.

The Glastonbury kitchen is one of the great medieval buildings and other vanished abbot's kitchens may have been almost as magnificent. But most monastic kitchens, tucked away in a corner of the cloister or precinct, were far simpler, in keeping with the very basic food produced in them, and in their way more evocative of the life lived by the majority of monks and nuns.

THE LAVER, THE REREDORTER AND THEIR WATER SUPPLY

Sanitary arrangements were very different in the Middle Ages from the way they are today. Bathrooms were unknown and so was running water, at least as far as the lay population was concerned. If you wanted to wash in warm water you had to heat it over the fire and carry it in a bowl or pail. Many people probably got their best bath in the local river. Latrines were also basic, ranging from a secluded pit in the ground to the castle garderobe discharging into the moat.

Monasteries aimed for more sophistication than this, taking great pains to provide the best the Middle Ages could manage when it came to a clean water supply and decent drainage. A large abbey – with its church, cloister and host of precinct structures – was the most complex type of building known in the Middle Ages, and founders went to huge lengths to find sites that could tap a good source of clean water and deliver this water wherever in the precinct it was needed. Local streams were often diverted so that clean water could run into the precinct at the upstream end while dirty water and waste could be discharged downstream. Separate facilities for the main part of the abbey, the infirmary and, in the later Middle Ages, the head of the house often meant quite complex channels for fresh water and drainage. The water often ran in stone-vaulted culverts, which were some of the most impressive engineering works of the period.

Remains of these culverts and channels can be found at many monastic sites. The Cistercians especially were renowned water engineers. At sites such as Kirkstall and Hailes, drains are visible at the surface, meticulously lined with finely cut stones and disappearing underground as barrel-vaulted tunnels linking the various parts of the precinct that needed a water supply. These waterworks are as impressive – if not so vast – as the great Victorian sewers. Today they are easy to miss, but they were just as vital to the communities they served as were the soaring Gothic arches and elaborate chapter houses.

These monastic waterworks were set within a larger context. Many houses – especially the Cistercian abbeys that held large country estates devoted to sheep farming – had mills that were driven by water. If one looks beyond the immediate precinct of the abbey, the waterworks often include canals, channels and ponds that supplied water mills – evidence for such buildings can be found at many Cistercian sites. Sometimes, the needs of the community changed – perhaps another mill was built or there was a new grant of land. In such cases a river, already diverted, might be re-routed again. Once more, the organisation and needs of the monastery are revealed in the planning. Earthworks in the fields around a ruined abbey often indicate the routes of former canals, drains and diverted streams. The landscape archaeology involved in studying this evidence and assessing the impact of monasteries on the countryside is a large field in its own right.

But nearer the heart of the monastery, the water supply provided the potential for better personal hygiene in the monastic community than amongst the laity. Fresh water for washing was channelled to the laver (or lavatorium). This washing place took the form of a lead-lined stone trough into which fresh water ran at one end and from which waste was discharged at the other. It was usually placed in the cloister, near the refectory, and the monks or nuns would wash at the laver before eating, for it was important to be both ritually and physically clean before the solemn occasion of the communal meal.

The most beautiful of all monastic washing places is at Gloucester,

Many ruined abbeys retain the remains of stone drains, like this one from the reredorter at Kirkham Priory.

The washing place at Kirkham is topped with a pair of arches and backed with decorative tracery of the late 13th century.

where the laver is built into its own compact passage parallel to the cloister walk. This beautiful space is roofed with a miniature version of the fan vaulting used in the main cloister and walled with stone carved in the Perpendicular style. It is high-status architecture for a washroom, testimony both to the importance of Gloucester's abbey and to the significance of washing as both literal and ritual cleansing. Other surviving lavers, such as the 13th-century one at Kirkham and the early 14th-century example at Norwich, are also built with care and elegance.

Monastic latrines were housed in a building known as the reredorter. This was often reached, as its name suggests, from the dormitory (or dorter) and was tucked away behind it, often also near to the infirmary. Reredorters were often quite substantial buildings. The one at Canterbury Cathedral Priory, for example, contained 55 separate cubicles. But even more impressive was their engineering. A special channel was often provided to bring flowing water from the abbey stream through the basement of the reredorter to flush away the waste material. Sometimes, as at Fountains, the reredorter was actually built over the stream itself.

The reredorter at Rievaulx is of three storeys, with the latrine seats themselves upstairs. The monks would have sat on wooden seats and were separated from each other by wooden partitions, the presence of which is implied by remaining gaps in the masonry of the walls. Waste material plunged through a void to the drain, which was at cellar level. Continuously running water flushed the waste out of the precinct and into the River Rye. The reredorter at Rievaulx and its accompanying drains form just one example of the way the monastic orders made sophisticated provision for the most basic human needs and functions.

ABBOTS' AND ABBESSES' LODGINGS

The head of a monastery usually had separate accommodation from the rest of the community and these lodgings got larger and more elaborate towards the later Middle Ages. The traditional position for the abbot's lodgings was on the western range of the cloister, where there would be a parlour or day room, a bedchamber, a dining room and a chapel for his use. This layout was followed in many Benedictine and Augustinian houses up to the 12th century. However, Cistercian monasteries were

This relief carving of Christ calling St Peter adorned the laver at Wenlock Priory.

Cells at the Carthusian monastery of Mount Grace had their own garderobes like this one. It was connected to an open drain that was flushed by a spring.

usually arranged differently. The lay brothers were accommodated in the western range and, in the 12th century, in keeping with the austerity of the order, the abbot was expected to sleep in the dormitory with the rest of the monks.

From the early 13th century onwards, abbots' lodgings began to change and get larger. Occasionally, as at Castle Acre Priory, the lodgings of the head of the house could expand to take over the entire western range of the cloister. Sometimes, as at Bardney Abbey, a whole collection of extra extensions was built on to the western range to provide extra accommodation for the abbot.

But there was often not enough room on the western range for this kind of expanded accommodation and so separate abbots' houses began to be built, away from the cloister. At Rievaulx and Furness former infirmaries were converted into abbots' houses in the later Middle Ages, while at Kirkstall a guest house became the hall house of the abbot. These buildings could resemble sizeable manor houses, with a large hall, together with rooms for the abbots' guests as well as private chambers and a chapel. Many of these abbots' houses also had their own kitchens.

The hall of a large abbot's house was arranged like that of a contemporary manor house – the kind of layout still seen in the halls of Oxford and Cambridge colleges today. At one end of the long room was a slightly raised dais for the table where the abbot ate with his most

The abbot's hall at Haughmond is a grand structure with a six-light bay window of the late 15th century.

important guests. A nearby doorway led to the abbot's private rooms and a large window lit the high table. Other tables, for lesser guests and retainers, were arranged lengthways in the main body of the hall. At the end opposite the dais was a wooden screen concealing an entrance passage that in a large monastery would also lead to the abbot's kitchen and to service rooms such as the pantry.

The ruined prior's lodging at Finchale Priory, dating mostly from the 13th century, gives a good idea of the kind of layout in such a building. A long prior's hall stands next to another large room, the prior's private chamber. Off this lead two smaller rooms: a chapel and what was probably the prior's study. The main rooms stand above a large vaulted undercroft. It is a large building and was probably still well used when Finchale became a holiday retreat for the monks of Durham in the 14th century.

Critics of the monasteries could find a lot to complain about in the size and grandeur of these heads' houses. Monks were meant to live in austerity, not dine in state. But the abbot of a large monastery was an important person, often involved in matters of church and state politics, and frequently he would have to entertain guests of high rank. Princely visitors expected a good reception.

While some monastic heads must have enjoyed the comfort and spaciousness of their lodgings, there is evidence that some did not. The priors of Bridlington, for example, were forced by the archbishops of York to keep a more lavish lodging than they wanted to, so that the archbishops had somewhere suitable to stay when visiting parishes in the eastern part of their province.

Abbots' houses have sometimes survived because they were recyclable domestic buildings that could form the basis of a private house after the dissolution. At Buildwas Abbey, for example, the abbot's lodgings, which were quite extensive, were adapted to create part of a Tudor house built on the site by the Grey family. This house later fell into decline, becoming a farmstead, but parts of the medieval structure remain. The prior's lodging at Wenlock Priory is another example of a monastic head's accommodation being converted to form an impressive private house.

But sometimes more of the medieval fabric remains – for example at Muchelney Abbey. Muchelney was a small abbey (the maximum number

At Muchelney Abbey the abbot's house has a parlour with several fine late medieval details. The fireplace is carved as beautifully as that in any medieval manor house.

of monks it housed was 20) and the surviving rooms in the abbot's lodging are mostly quite small. But the quality of the workmanship is high, with carved wooden panelling, coffered wooden ceilings and fine stone fireplaces and other carved remains. Much of it dates from the early 16th century and it provided a serviceable and fashionable home for the family who took it over when the abbey was dissolved.

DISCIPLINE

For a monastery to work effectively it had to be well disciplined. The abbot and his deputy, the prior, were responsible for enforcing discipline. In some monasteries there was also an obedientiary called the claustral prior, whose duty it was to make the rounds of the monastery and check that no one was breaking the rule. He was expected to pay special attention to the dark, out-of-the-way parts of the monastery, such as crypts or undercrofts, where infringements of the rule might otherwise pass unnoticed. Any wrongdoers would be reported in chapter and would expect a punishment to be handed out.

For such a system to work, the head of the monastery had to be beyond reproach. Problems could arise if an abbot was too lax – and also if he was too strict or if his punishments were arbitrary. In the

13th century, for example, the monks of St Albans had a dispute with their abbot, William of Trumpington, complaining about his habit of sending brothers into exile and his tendency to associate too freely with the lay population.

The Cistercians, as an austere and reforming order, realised the importance of discipline and that it was vital to build disciplinary procedure into every level of the monastic hierarchy. Therefore they built into their governance a system of visitations and general chapters (*see* p 38) that was designed to impose good discipline throughout the order. All abbots were expected to attend an annual general chapter at Cîteaux and all monasteries were to be visited every year by the abbot of their mother house.

This system was not without its problems. Abbots from far-flung places such as northern England and Wales could have difficulty in travelling to France, especially in times of war. And King Edward I actually banned abbots from attending general chapter in 1298, fearful that the money they carried to pay for their board and lodgings might fall into the hands of his enemies. Visitation could also be a problem, especially for a large abbey with many daughter houses. But in spite of these difficulties, the system of general chapter and visitation gave the Cistercian order the machinery to enforce discipline.

Soon, other orders, such as the Premonstratensians and friars, were recognising the merits of this and introducing similar systems. The Gilbertines appointed scrutators who visited each monastery every year. The Benedictines and Augustinian canons began to hold provincial chapters from the early 13th century onwards. And to promote good discipline further, the Fourth Lateran Council in 1215 ordered the bishops to work towards improving the monasteries in their dioceses.

Records of visitations are patchy, but bishops and monastic visitors unearthed a variety of faults. There were complaints that monks and nuns were not observing the rule of silence, that they had private property, that visitors or guests of the opposite sex had been allowed into the monastery, that services were rushed through too quickly and that meat was being eaten.

Various punishments could be imposed on monks or nuns who stepped out of line in these ways: for example fasting on bread and vegetables on certain days, labouring on a monastic farm and keeping

Beating was a common punishment in medieval monasteries and this medieval scourge from Rievaulx, made of plaited bronze chainwork, is a rare surviving example.

strictly to church and cloister for a set period. Corporal punishment was also used quite frequently. Missing the office might result in a period of fasting. Unauthorised absence from the precinct might be punished with a beating. In an especially serious case there might be a number of punishments. A well-known example from the York records is a monk of Monk Bretton called William de Wadworth, whose sentence was summarised by the historian David Knowles in his book *The Religious Orders in England*: 'he was to take the lowest place in choir, cloister, dormitory and refectory; on Wednesdays and Fridays he was to fast on bread and vegetables; he was to follow the strictest observance, not to go out, and not to celebrate Mass'. And all this was to take place at Whitby, where the sinner was sent in exile.

Occasionally, in extreme cases, a monk might be locked up in a punishment cell and made to endure a diet of bread and water. But abbots seem to have been aware of the potentially damaging effects of solitary confinement and often instructed members of the monastery to visit prisoners regularly and to be friendly in their manner when visiting. Most abbeys probably had a punishment cell for this purpose, but the architectural remains of these small rooms are slight. One example is

The priory prison at Mount Grace is in one corner of the cloister. There was originally one small room on each of the three floors.

found at Mount Grace Priory, where a compact three-story prison is located in the south-west corner of the main cloister. In a sense, the most clear architectural reminders of monastic discipline are the many surviving gatehouses, which stand as symbols of the way in which monks spent most of their lives confined within the precinct under the watchful eye of abbot and prior.

THE INFIRMARY

The only properly educated people in the Middle Ages were the clergy and many monks and priests used their learning to study and practise medicine. Even one pope, John XXI (1276–7), was a physician and wrote a book on medicine, *Thesaurus Pauperum* (*Treasury of the Poor*). St Benedict realised that the ability to heal the sick squared perfectly with the Christian duty to help others and included healing in the rule: 'The care of the sick is to be placed above and before every other duty, as if indeed Christ were being directly served by waiting on them.'

Many monasteries became centres of health care. Some were healing shrines, where pilgrims were said to have benefited from miraculous cures. The most famous was at the cathedral-priory of Canterbury, where

This reconstruction shows the infirmary cloister at Rievaulx in about 1250.

pilgrimage to the shrine of St Thomas Becket was said to cure blindness, leprosy and deafness. But almost all sacred relics had healing properties attributed to them.

However, medieval medicine was not based solely on the healing power of religious relics. Monks in continental Europe translated many of the Arabic texts in which the medical wisdom of the ancient Greeks was preserved. This knowledge, together with traditional cures using herbal medicine, circulated through the monasteries as monks travelled from one house to another or as books were copied in scriptoria. Thus medieval medicine was a mixture of superstition and astrology on the one hand and time-honoured cures and good sense on the other. A sick monk or nun had a better chance than most in the Middle Ages of finding a cure.

When monks or nuns fell ill, or when they got too old and frail to withstand the full rigours of monastic life, they were sent to the infirmary. This was the domain of the infirmarer, an obedientiary who was expected to be good-humoured, kind and gentle toward his charges and who would be skilled in caring for the sick, though in a larger house he might have a physician to help him. The infirmarer would have to keep a well-stocked cupboard of herbal remedies, keep a fire going in all but the warmest weather and provide light and comfort for the sick and old in his care. He would sing the canonical hours on behalf of those who could not manage the duty for themselves and would pray for the sick. And he would keep the rest of the monastic community updated on their progress so that, for example, the appropriate vigil could be mounted for a patient who was thought to be close to death.

The more comfortable life available in the infirmary was attractive to many. Though the rule of St Benedict forbade the eating of meat, an exception could be made for the sick. The diet in the infirmary was more attractive than the regime of vegetable dishes and bread endured by those who had to eat in the refectory (*see* pp 113–14). In addition, those in the infirmary might be allowed to get up later and to walk in the monastery gardens when other colleagues were at work. As time went on, the rule was relaxed in many houses, so that monks were allowed regular 'holidays' from the harsh regime of the monastery to eat meat in another room – often the dining room of the infirmary.

One such break from the regular monastic routine came when monks

The infirmary at Halesowen has survived because it was used as a barn after the dissolution.

went to the infirmary for blood-letting. This practice was thought to be beneficial to the health and so was done regularly. It was eagerly anticipated because it gave the patient access to the easier life of the infirmary. As a result, the orders stipulated that one should go for blood-letting only a set number of times per year (Augustinian canons were allowed to go eight times a year, whereas Cistercians were limited to four). A three-day rest in the infirmary followed each blood-letting session.

By the late Middle Ages the attractions of such breaks from routine were strong. In houses such as Westminster, monks took it in turns to eat meat – at any one time, half the community ate in the refectory and the other half enjoyed a more luxurious diet. On feast days, the diet was still better, with delicacies such as salmon and eel accompanied by wine. And in some monasteries, there were reports of monks abandoning the refectory completely in favour of the more flavoursome and varied diet of the infirmary or some other secondary dining room.

The infirmary where all this took place was a complex of buildings within the monastic precinct but usually slightly apart from the cloister, often a little towards the east. The exact location varied – the priorities were to keep the complex away from any hustle and bustle and to provide it with a fresh water supply and drainage. The infirmary was like a miniature monastery within the main establishment. At its heart was a large hall, where the infirm spent their nights and much of their days; nearby was a chapel, a kitchen, a washing place, a lavatory and a dining room.

Infirmaries varied quite a lot in layout. Some were made up of a cluster of buildings; occasionally, as at Waverley, the infirmary buildings were arranged around their own small cloister. At the Augustinian abbey at Haughmond, the infirmary and abbot's lodgings occupy one range of a second cloister, a very unusual arrangement. A row of tall, twin-light windows with elegant tracery indicates that Haughmond's infirmary hall was an impressive room – many other abbeys made do with much plainer accommodation. There were also variations in size. Fountains, a large and well-appointed monastery, had an infirmary hall about 175ft (53m) in length. Smaller houses had smaller halls.

Infirmaries also changed over time. Originally most halls were probably arranged rather like modern hospital wards with rows of beds. But in the later Middle Ages, infirmary halls, like monastic dormitories, were often divided up into lots of small chambers to provide individual rooms for the inmates. The infirmary hall at Fountains is a good example. It began in the 13th century as an open-plan aisled hall. But by the following century, the spaces between the pillars were partitioned off to make a series of private chambers, many with their own fireplaces.

Netley Abbey's infirmary still stands to gable height, giving a good idea of the scale of the building.

Sometimes the site of an infirmary changed as the needs of the community developed. At Furness, for example, the original infirmary hall was converted to provide lodgings for the abbot in the early 14th century and a new infirmary was built. This was larger and more impressive than the original, with a hall some 126ft (38m) long, with rows of recesses to take the heads of the inmates' beds. There was a vaulted chapel (still well preserved) and an octagonal kitchen.

Patients in the infirmary benefited both from greater privacy and more comfort as a result of changes like this. Similar alterations were made at other houses, including Beaulieu and Kirkstall. They were part of the general movement towards comfort and relaxing of the rule which is seen for many aspects of monastic life in the later Middle Ages. But there was also a therapeutic benefit. Patients in the relative luxury of a small room had more chance of recovery than those in big, draughty infirmary halls. And those who were in the infirmary to live out their last days could do so in greater comfort.

A carving from Muchelney shows a monk carrying bread and ale, which may have been provisions for one of the corrodians of the house.

Monastic infirmaries – of which there are interesting remains at Haughmond, Canterbury, Ely, Gloucester and Peterborough – were set up for the benefit of the monks or nuns of the house. Some lay people, such as guests or corrodians (pensioners who opted to leave their estates to an abbey in return for food and accommodation in their last years), might take advantage of the medical knowledge of the infirmarer. On the whole the infirmary was a hospital for the religious community, but the outside community must have also benefited.

MONASTIC HOSPITALS

Many towns had hospitals to care for the lay population and several of these were run by monks or nuns. The Augustinian canons were notable providers of health care – their regime, which encouraged pastoral work and shunned the cloistered seclusion of the traditional orders, allowed them to go out more into the community. Both St Thomas's and St Bartholomew's hospitals in London were originally run by the Augustinians; they also ran two hospitals in Cirencester. There were many other such establishments run by the canons, to the extent that the terms 'priory' and 'hospital' can become confused.

The hospital of St Cross at Winchester is one of the most elaborate medieval hospitals, with one range of accommodation for the inmates and another containing the master's house.

One order, the Knights of the Hospital of St John of Jerusalem, known as the Hospitallers, were established specifically to care for sick and poor pilgrims who were travelling to the holy places of Jerusalem after it was captured by Christian crusaders in 1099. Like the other military orders that began during the crusading period, they established themselves back home in western Europe and they ran a number of hospitals in England. One of the most famous early hospitals – St Cross in Winchester – was founded by Bishop Henry of Blois in the 12th century. The bishop entrusted it to the Hospitallers to run.

Like monastic infirmaries, these institutions took on a dual role of caring for the old and healing the sick. Thus a medieval establishment could be more like an almshouse or care-home than a modern hospital – which is why many early almshouses are referred to as hospitals.

In addition to these mostly urban hospitals run by monks or nuns, there were also establishments built as isolation hospitals for lepers. London's St Giles in the Fields and Rochester's St Bartholomew's were both leper hospitals run by monasteries. They tried to be rigorous in keeping sufferers isolated from the rest of the population – a policy that eventually led to the eradication of leprosy in Britain – even though the disease was not well understood and other skin diseases were often confused with it. Though life expectancy was much lower in the Middle Ages than it is today, the monasteries played a key part in helping the curable live longer and bringing comfort to those in their last years.

THE GUEST HALL

The rule of St Benedict required that monasteries offer hospitality to visitors as if they were Christ himself. As St Benedict put it: 'Let all guests that come be received like Christ, for he will say: "I was a stranger and ye took me in." And let fitting honour be shown to all, but especially to churchmen and pilgrims.' And he went on to stress the special attention that should be given to the poor: the rich will always command attention, but in the poor 'is Christ more truly welcomed'. In an age when there were no hotels, when travel was difficult and dangerous, and where inns were scarce outside towns, the provision of hospitality was a vital, if taxing, job. Abbeys usually had a guest hall where visitors could be accommodated and this building was presided over by an important obedientiary, the guest master.

People travelled much less in the Middle Ages than they do today. But there were plenty of people on the move who needed putting up for the night. Craft workers, such as a master mason travelling to work on a new cathedral, messengers carrying letters for kings or lords, clergy on similar

Elegant blind arcading marks the guest chambers at Easby Abbey.

errands for their bishops, merchants en route to fairs, small armies of pilgrims making for great shrines such as Canterbury or Hailes – all could prevail on monastic hospitality.

Travelling monks or nuns were less common – they were expected to spend most of their lives in and around the monastery. But if a member of the regular clergy turned up, he or she would usually stay with the brothers or sisters in the dormitory and would expect to take part in the life of the monastery, observing the canonical hours and playing a full role in the liturgy.

The laity would make their way to the guest hall, which would be their base and sleeping place while they enjoyed the abbey's hospitality. For meals, they would most likely join the abbot, either at his table in the refectory or, later, when abbots took to living separately from the monks, in the abbot's hall. It was customary for the cellarer to receive and entertain visiting clergy, though no doubt the abbot would also meet them, for he would be anxious to hear any news about church business that he could glean from those passing through his house.

The guest master was responsible for running the guest hall, making sure food was available for guests and overseeing the stabling of their horses. It could be an onerous job and demanded a specific skill set – combining the ability to deal with a wide variety of people with the organisation needed to ensure a good supply of food and the smooth running of facilities – more often found in hoteliers than in monks. And this was appropriate, for the guest master was running what was virtually a hotel.

But the big difference was that the guests did not pay for their keep. Anyone could turn up and expect hospitality and guests could range from a powerful lord and his retinue, who expected a certain degree of comfort and good stabling, to a lowly traveller on foot who was grateful for a bed. The biggest strain on resources came when there was a major local festival – for example a saint's day that attracted pilgrims or a big fair – or when a large household arrived.

To save monasteries from undue strain, one or two restrictions were imposed on the hospitality on offer. There were limits, for example, on the number of horses a guest might bring with him, or the monastery might impose a limit on the total number of guests it could accommodate during any one year. Another restriction – intended to protect the moral well-being of the monks or nuns rather than the financial health of the monastery – was that guests should normally be of the same sex as the inhabitants of the monastery. But this rule could be relaxed, especially when a couple were travelling together, and some big houses had separate guest halls for men and women.

Patrons were the most privileged of all monastic guests. No patron would be turned away, even if he or she was of the opposite sex to the inhabitants of the house. Even the Cistercians, who as one of the strictest of orders normally excluded women completely from their communities, would make an exception for a female patron, though she was only allowed to stay for one night. Even to be the relative or successor of a patron seems to have given some the right to claim special privileges. For example a 12th-century bishop of Coventry assumed that he should be accommodated at Buildwas Abbey because it was founded by a previous bishop of the diocese (or see).

Guests were often accommodated in rooms on the upper floor of the cloister's western range. There were good reasons for putting the guests here. The western range was the nearest to the entrance and great court of the monastery, so it was easy for guests to find. The west range was also relatively far from the monks' dormitory, the chapter house and other areas where distractions would be unwelcome. Alternatively, the guest accommodation could be in the same block as the abbot's or prior's lodgings (which might themselves be in the western range or in some other position). Or the monastery might build an entirely separate guest hall somewhere within the abbey precinct, usually within the outer court.

The guest hall could be one of the largest buildings in a monastery. At Cluny in France there were beds for 45 male guests and 30 women, plus additional accommodation for poorer travellers who arrived on foot. Durham, another large monastery, had an impressive guest hall, described in the Middle Ages as 'a goodly brave place much like unto the body of a church with verey fair pillers supporting yt on ether side and in the mydest of the haule a most large Raunge for the fyer'. Next to it were private chambers, including one, known as the king's chamber and said to be well named. Guests would expect to be well treated here and they were not disappointed, enjoying good food at the prior's table.

The description of the church-like guest hall at Durham gives a clue to its structure: it would have been a large aisled hall. No doubt it had a service wing at one end and private chambers at the other as a contemporary manor house or a large abbot's house would have done. Accommodating high-status guests was obviously also a priority for the monks at Fountains. In the 12th century they built a pair of fine guest houses. These were each divided horizontally, to provide spacious and separate living accommodation in ground and upper floors so that four high-status guests could stay there at a time.

Not all guest halls would have been as grand as this and Fountains, a large monastery, also had a hall for poorer travellers. Elsewhere, the

The guest house at Fountains Abbey was a large building detached from the main abbey complex and accessed from the great court to the west of the cloister and church.

priority was often to provide a communal hall for a large number of guests. Many of these halls were upgraded during the Middle Ages as the numbers of guests increased or there was more demand for separate accommodation for rich and high-ranking travellers. Archaeologists have traced the development of the guest hall at Kirkstall, which began as a timber-framed aisled hall in the early 13th century. It was rebuilt in stone later in the 13th century, with the addition of extra chambers and a separate timber-framed western hall for poorer guests. The complex was rebuilt yet again in the 15th century, with further chamber space. In this final transformation the western hall was rebuilt and much of it was given over to stables. This succession of alterations and rebuildings indicates that hospitality was important to the monastery and that generations of abbots wanted to provide the right kind of accommodation. Enshrined as it was in the rule, hospitality was taken very seriously indeed.

The right kind of provision in Cistercian monasteries went one step further. The Cistercians did not normally allow the laity to worship in their churches, so in their abbeys a special chapel had to be provided for guests. This was traditionally built at the abbey gates. Such a chapel has survived at Kirkstead in Lincolnshire, where it is the only substantial remaining structure of the Cistercian abbey. It is a small building but built to high architectural standards with a vaulted ceiling, a feature rarely found outside large churches and cathedrals. The ribs of the vault rest on corbels richly carved with the stylised 'stiff-leaf' decoration fashionable when the chapel was built in around 1240. The bosses, the carved stones where the ribs intersect, are also carved with stiff leaf and the one at the east end has the lamb of God. The pairs and trios of lancet windows are flanked by slender shafts, those at the east end once more topped with stiff-leaf capitals. The whole chapel is a superb example of the best building style of the mid-13th century, by which time the Cistercians, who had resisted architectural ornament in favour of an austere, otherworldly architecture, had relaxed their views somewhat.

In some places, part of the work of hospitality was farmed out to an inn that was built by the monastery and let to a tenant. Monasteries often held extensive lands and for orders like the Benedictines, who had many abbeys in towns and cities, ownership of an inn was a way of earning

income and providing extra hospitality. Locations on pilgrimage routes or in towns that were themselves places of pilgrimage were obvious sites.

Therefore a number of early inns were monastic foundations. The George in Winchcombe, Gloucestershire, was founded by the abbot of Winchcombe Abbey, Richard Kidderminster, in the late 15th century. It was well placed to serve not just visitors to Kidderminster's own monastery, but also the many pilgrims to the nearby Cistercian house at Hailes with its shrine containing the 'blood of Christ'. This 'George' is no longer an inn, but another George, at Norton St Philip in Somerset, still offers hospitality. It was the possession of the monks of Hinton Charterhouse, who used it successively as a wool store, guest house and inn. The numerous other monastic inns include the Star in Oxford (belonging to Osney Abbey), the George at Glastonbury and the New Inn at Gloucester. Many similar establishments took monastic hospitality into another sphere beyond the abbey gatehouse.

The George Inn at Norton St Philip has a stone lower floor of the 14th and 15th centuries, with timber-framed 16th-century upper storeys.

THE PRECINCT AND GATEHOUSE

It is not so obvious now, but in the Middle Ages the first thing to strike a visitor to an abbey was that it was an enclave, a place apart, walled off from the rest of the world. Monasteries had substantial outer walls with a main gate through which everyone entering – on foot, mounted or with a cart – had to pass. Once inside, the visitor would be faced with a variety of buildings, mostly the working structures – barns, granaries, stables and so on – that helped the abbey to be as self-sufficient as it could. Nearby there would also be the abbey guest hall and not far beyond would be the focus of the community: the abbey church with its collection of buildings where the monks or nuns worked, ate, slept and, above all, worshipped.

An aerial photograph of St Benet's Abbey shows the outline of the precinct, traces of the foundations of various precinct structures and fragments of a monastic building.

Some monasteries were more substantially walled than others. Strong walls were especially important if the house was in a potential battle zone. Abbeys and priories in the far north, such as Alnwick and Hulne, invested in solid precinct walls when there was a threat of attack from the Scots. And in the far south of England, similar precautions were taken during the Hundred Years War. From Quarr on the Isle of Wight to abbeys such as Battle in East Sussex, licence was granted to put up solid fortified walls to resist potential attacks from the French and the pirates and raiders who might come in their wake.

Curtain walls remain at some monasteries, such as Hulne, and at Michelham there is even a protective moat. But the most outstanding evidence of the policing, as it were, of the monastic precinct is the large number of gatehouses that remain, many of them striking and substantial buildings in their own right. One of the finest and earliest is the Norman tower of St James at Bury St Edmunds, actually one of two gatehouses that survive as the main remains of this once-great Benedictine abbey. This tower was built during the first half of the 12th century as a dual-purpose building – it is both the belfry of the adjoining parish church of St James and the gateway to the abbey precinct. Its round arches and openings are typical of Norman building and the whole structure is monumental and in every way worthy of what was once a huge abbey. Other Norman gates, such as the slightly later one to the Augustinian abbey at Bristol (now the cathedral), are just as magnificent though less tall. The Bristol gatehouse has a rich complement of Norman mouldings in zigzag, nailhead and spiral patterns on its arches.

There are still more abbey gatehouses from the later Middle Ages, many of them almost as strong and imposing as the entrances to medieval castles. Many were rebuilt or strengthened to provide extra security in times of strife. The one at Battle dates from the late 1330s, a period when there was a distinct threat of invasion from France during the Hundred Years War. Bury's second gatehouse was built and fortified in 1346 in response to rioting a few years earlier. The gatehouse at Thornton followed in the 1380s, when the Peasants' Revolt was still fresh in the memory. And monastic gatehouse-building continued through the 15th century, producing, for example, a remodelled entrance building at Cleeve and the gatehouse at Kingswood, which is virtually all that remains of that Cistercian house.

This Norman tower at Bury St Edmunds makes the grandest of abbey gatehouses.

The gatehouse of Kingswood Abbey has pinnacles, niches and a vaulted entrance way. These features show that this was once a rich abbey, although hardly any of its other buildings survive.

Though their architectural style evolved with the centuries, most of these gatehouses have a similar layout. The gate itself on the ground floor is wide enough for a cart to pass through. Sometimes there is a smaller doorway to admit those on foot when the large gate is barred to horses and vehicles; sometimes this function would have been fulfilled with a little 'gate within the gate' for pedestrians. Usually there would have been a small window or grating through which visitors could be scrutinised before being granted admission when the gate was closed. To the side of the main gate would be a room for the porter, the person who would keep an eye on all comings and goings, to make sure that visitors were directed to the guest hall or, if appropriate, to the abbot or abbess. With supplies also coming in, artisans entering to do building or repair work and, in some houses, a stream of pilgrims, the porter's job could be a busy one.

The gatehouse at Wetheral survived because it was used as a vicarage in the 16th and 17th centuries, before being used for storing hay.

Most gatehouses had at least one room above the entrance way. This room could fulfil a variety of functions – courts or schools took place in some, while others contained prisons, offices or extra guest accommodation. Some, like the imposing gatehouse at Thornton, had large chambers with private rooms off them; they might even have their own fireplaces and garderobes. Perhaps chambers like these were for important guests or corrodians.

Monastic gatehouses have survived in large numbers and it is not difficult to see why. For a start, the gatehouse was on the edge of its monastic precinct and, for urban monasteries, this often meant being in the middle of a town. Therefore many gatehouses were conveniently sited for some secular use. They were strong buildings by definition and the accommodation above the gate could be useful – the lay beneficiaries of the dissolution must have seized on them as ready-made and readily usable stone buildings. Rooms of the type found at Thornton were already designed for residential use; others could be converted for this.

Gatehouses were also often handsome buildings – they frequently look as if they were built to impress outsiders as well as to keep the precinct secure. Thus there was an added attraction in keeping a gatehouse and converting it to secular use. From Gothic gatehouses like the one at Canterbury to elaborate essays in local architectural style like the example at St Osyth's Priory with its walls of patterned flint, from showpieces of carving like Ramsey's to the simpler gatehouse (once used as the local vicarage) at Wetheral Priory, monastic gatehouses are some of our most notable buildings.

WORKING BUILDINGS

At a monastic site it is usually easy to find the church, the cloister and the buildings that lead off the cloister walks. At many sites, at least some of these buildings still have some standing walls; if not, archaeologists have often revealed the foundations in their excavations. When we have looked at these buildings we have seen the real core of the monastery: the scene of daily worship; the buildings where the monastic community cooked, ate, slept, washed, discussed business, wrote and read; and the places where they went when they were ill, felt cold or needed to consult their superior. But a monastery was much more than this. Surrounding the church and cloister of a typical monastery was a walled precinct full of mostly utilitarian buildings connected with farming, food supply, building maintenance and other tasks. And beyond the walls there could be numerous monastic farms.

Most of these working buildings are little noticed by visitors, though they have been studied by scholars. They are often less architecturally glamorous than churches or chapter houses and many have been obliterated, their stones recycled after the dissolution to leave little more than earthworks in the ground where their foundations remain. Such remains are a rich field for the landscape archaeologist, with evidence showing up on aerial photographs or when a low sun casts dramatic shadows across the fields.

Other structures were taken over by lay owners in Tudor times and were subsequently rebuilt so that little or nothing remains of the original structures. But interesting remnants survive of barns and granaries, breweries and bakehouses, mills and woolhouses, forges and storehouses, and these illustrate how important monasteries were to the economy of the Middle Ages.

These buildings are usually examples of vernacular architecture – buildings constructed using local labour, in the customary style of the area and with local materials. Barns, for example, were usually timber-framed in Essex but built of stone in the Cotswolds – both types seem an integral part of their local landscapes and almost as natural as the stands of trees or outcrops of rocks that provided their raw materials. Like the traditional farm buildings that still survive all over the countryside today, these structures were not built to be impressive but to fulfil a specific function. Because of their sheer size and the artfulness with which they are built, some of these – especially the big monastic barns – are the most imposing buildings of the Middle Ages.

Great barns

The largest building on a medieval farm was usually the barn and monastic farms were no exception. Big farmyard barns were used mainly for storing corn, which was brought in sheaves from the fields.

Prior's Hall Barn, Widdington, is a fine monastic structure, its weatherboarded walls typical of traditional farm buildings in Essex. Widdington belonged to the French monastery of St-Valery-sur-Somme after the Norman conquest, but the present barn was probably built in the 15th century for New College, Oxford.

They were often enormous structures. The great barn at Cholsey, belonging to Reading Abbey, was 303ft (92m) in length. This was the longest known medieval barn, but was sadly demolished in 1815. However, there are many survivors over 100ft (30m) long. These buildings were designed with great practicality, usually with walls pierced with slits for ventilation and also with holes to encourage owls, valued hunters of mice and other vermin.

A large barn usually had an entrance big enough to take the farm's largest cart, so that a load of sheaves could be brought in without extra handling. There was usually another doorway opposite the main entrance, making a cross-passage which was paved; larger barns could have two such cross-passages. This was a practical arrangement when unloading, because it meant that the cart could drive in one door and out the other, without the need to turn round. The cross-passage had another use: it was also the farm's threshing floor. There was usually also a large porch, to shelter a cart waiting for another to unload.

Many monastic barns have disappeared. Beaulieu Abbey, for example, had 27 barns at the dissolution. Of these, only the one at Great Coxwell remains; however, it is one of the most magnificent of all monastic buildings. The great 19th-century designer and writer William Morris said that the barn at Great Coxwell was 'as beautiful as a cathedral'.

He recognised the extraordinary elegance and economy of its design and was no doubt awestruck, like every modern visitor, by the high interior, the roof supported on rows of posts to produce a church-like space with a 'nave' and two 'aisles'. The construction of the roof itself, with its network of rafters, braces and purlins, is a triumph of carpentry.

There are many other barns almost as beautiful as Great Coxwell – for example the great timber-framed barley barn of around 1220 at Temple Cressing and its neighbouring wheat barn; the long stone barn at Abbotsbury, once a rival in length to Cholsey but now much shorter; and the magnificent stone barn at Bradford-on-Avon, part of a collection of buildings belonging to the estate farm of Shaftesbury Abbey.

This magnificent stone-built barn with its oak-beamed roof in Bradford-on-Avon was built to hold produce belonging to the abbey of Shaftesbury.

Woolhouses

In some parts of England, the most important aspect of monastic farming was the raising of sheep for wool. Sheep were farmed widely in upland areas and the Cistercians in particular, with their sizeable landholdings in areas such as Yorkshire, were large and successful sheep farmers.

Just as grain needed storing and processing, so did wool. Sheep farmers needed buildings where their fleeces could be stored, sorted, washed and packed. These woolhouses had to be clean and secure, so they were often substantial stone buildings. One that belonged to Beaulieu Abbey still stands in Southampton. A plain, business-like building, it looks rather like a medieval warehouse, which is basically what it was.

The remains of another woolhouse have been excavated at Fountains Abbey. This was a building, existing mainly as low walls and foundations, that had been identified as a bakehouse in the 1880s. The remains were reinterpreted as the result of an excavation by Glyn Coppack in the late 1970s. Like many monastic buildings, the woolhouse had been through a series of reconstructions, but by the early 14th century it consisted of a substantial barn with an office, plus a fulling mill driven by an undershot water wheel. During the 14th century dye vats were installed, together with furnaces to heat water, and a partition wall was built to isolate the western aisles, which were probably used for cloth finishing. In the next century the building's use changed again, with remains of glass-working and smith's equipment indicating that it had been converted to form a number of workshops.

So the story of the Fountains woolhouse shows first that a monastery farming sheep on a large scale needed a substantial building to process and store wool, and second, that the needs of this particular monastery often changed and that its working buildings were altered and converted over the centuries as a result. While we are used to looking at the remains of, say, a monastic church, confident that it was used for worship throughout the Middle Ages, the history of a working building can be very different, changing with the times.

Dovecotes

Another building form that has survived in large numbers is the dovecote. Pigeons were an important source of meat in the Middle Ages and they were valued because they were easy to keep – the birds found their own food for most of the year and their keepers usually only needed to feed them in the depths of winter. They also fitted well into the monastic economy. Though monks and nuns in general were not supposed to eat meat, a monastery did have some demand for meat, for those in the infirmary or others enjoying a holiday from the usual rigours of the monastic diet.

The 14th-century dovecote at Kinwarton is probably a relic of a grange belonging to Evesham Abbey.

There were other advantages to keeping pigeons or doves; the feathers provided stuffing material for mattresses and the dung that could be gathered from the base of the dovecote was good for the garden and was also used in the preparation of parchment, an important consideration in a monastery.

Dovecotes come in various shapes and sizes, but the most common design is a compact round building. There is usually a conical roof topped with a louvered lantern, through which the birds could get in and out. An alternative design, found in western England, has a corbelled stone roof with a central hole. Inside, the walls are lined with nest holes and a device called a potence, a ladder mounted on a central turning pole, gives access to the holes. A round medieval dovecote at Kinwarton survives with its potence. The building belonged to Evesham Abbey from the mid-14th century. There are also square and rectangular dovecotes, like the one at Long Crendon belonging to Notley Abbey. It has more than 1,000 nest holes, making it one of the larger examples, an indication of how important pigeons and doves must have been to monastic life.

Mills

We think of the Middle Ages as a pre-industrial period. Most people lived in the country and worked the land, the monasteries ran great farms and everyone's status and power was gauged by the land that they held. But there were industries in the Middle Ages and some processes were powered by machinery. In most monasteries, machinery meant water power and water power meant mills.

Mills were used to power various processes. Grinding corn to make flour was essential: every monastery needed its daily bread. Where there were sheep farms, fulling mills were needed to process the wool. And mills could also be used to power machinery such as hammers for metalworking. Thus a mill was a key building in most monasteries and,

A post mill is shown on this carved relief from Rievaulx. The central post that supports the body of the mill, the steps and the four sails are clearly visible.

because of its importance to the monks' or nuns' staple diet, it was often sited in the precinct where there was also a supply of running water.

In addition, mills meant income. A landlord could rent a mill to a tenant or charge a farmer to grind corn. Therefore large abbeys, especially the Benedictine and Augustinian houses, owned many mills and did well out of them. In the 14th century, for example, the great abbey of Glastonbury had 27 water mills on its manors. The Cistercians, on the other hand, were not supposed to own mills as a source of income. Generally, their monasteries had one mill for grinding their own corn. But there were exceptions. For example when the order of Savigny merged with the Cistercian order in the 1140s, the Savigniacs were allowed to keep their mills.

A number of mills with a monastic history survive, but most of these were rebuilt or converted to some other use after the dissolution. Therefore the mill at Fountains Abbey – a roofed, three-storey building that was still grinding corn on the eve of the Second World War – is unusual. It is also unusually large – originally it was more than

A water wheel at the abbey mill at Fountains reminds us that the building was in use well after the dissolution.

A mill was a major feature of Bordesley Abbey. The triangular earthworks to the right of this picture are the remains of a millpond, while the brown area to the left represents the excavations of the mill building itself.

100ft (30m) in length and had a central chamber with a pair of undershot wheels. Most abbey mills were much smaller than this and many were probably timber buildings that have disappeared without trace. Others can be detected from the earthworks left behind by their foundations and their millponds – there is a good example at the Cistercian abbey of Hailes.

Other buildings

One could fill an entire book with information about the working buildings associated with monasteries. In effect it would be a history of medieval crafts and trades, so diverse were the activities of the monks, their servants and their tenants. One example is tanning, in which leather was treated by soaking for long periods in a solution containing oak bark. This is represented at Rievaulx Abbey by a set of tanning vats built of tiles, together with remains of a bark store, bark mill, tanner's house and other structures. Another is rabbit-keeping, demonstrated by surviving warreners' lodges and the earthworks of the warrens

This small medieval house was probably home to the gamekeeper or warrener of Thetford Priory. The prior had the right to hunt for small game, but the area was vulnerable to armed poachers, hence the defensive features of the building.

themselves. Metalworking, with its smithies and hammer mills, is a third. The various crafts of the building trade represent still more, for many abbeys were undergoing building work for decades and there were always building repairs required around the monastic precinct. A monastery was an entire world in miniature and its needs were as large and varied as those of a village or small town.

An illustration from the 14th-century Luttrell Psalter *shows rabbits and their burrows on a mound, perhaps an artificial rabbit warren.*

BEYOND THE PRECINCT

In the Middle Ages one way of measuring the influence of a person or institution was the amount of land they held. In the feudal system of landholding that prevailed after the Norman conquest, the king owned all the land, allocating large areas to prominent people or bodies in return for services. These key landholders might themselves parcel out smaller areas of land to tenants, again in return for goods or services, and so on down the social hierarchy.

Monasteries were some of the largest landholders in the Middle Ages. Their holdings were vast and widely scattered. The older Benedictine abbeys – foundations such as Glastonbury – were amongst the richest of them all. They tended to hold valuable, fertile land in lowland areas, they had a lot of it and for the most part it consisted of complete manors, so was conveniently parcelled together. A lot of it was treated as demesne land – in other words peasant tenants, supervised by an official known as a reeve, worked this land on behalf of the abbey. The rest was reserved for the tenants' own use to give them a supply of food and a possible source of extra profit.

The abbeys that were founded later did not get quite such a good deal. Later Benedictine and Augustinian abbeys, for example, tended to have smaller holdings and the land was scattered more widely. They made up for this by reclaiming land, turning ground of poor quality into land that would produce a better income. If their holdings were especially scattered, they could adopt more of a cash economy, selling produce near their farms, collecting the profits and using them to buy food for the monks from suppliers local to the abbey. Farming for profit became increasingly attractive in the later Middle Ages. In the late 12th and early 13th centuries, for example, prices increased and monasteries that were growing crops for sale found themselves well placed to exploit the higher prices.

Later still came many of the Cistercian foundations. They made a virtue of accepting land in isolated places, especially poor ground that others found hard to farm. These estates could be huge and the Cistcercians became famous as sheep farmers, taking advantage of livestock that did well on poorer, hilly land. But the white monks also farmed the crops that they needed to supply their refectories.

The friars rejected property, but still found themselves holding urban plots that could have gardens and large orchards. Thus even they became part of the medieval economy of farming and growing. So too did the military orders, who farmed on a large scale, ploughing the profits into their work in the East.

Most of these lands were used for farming. The monks were mixed farmers, adapting their produce both to their needs and to the land they held. In many cases their diet was vegetarian so they needed crops – wheat for bread, barley to brew beer and the peas, beans and other legumes that formed key ingredients in the pottage eaten in monasteries. Legumes were useful in other ways. They could be dried for storing and later use, they made good horse fodder and they fitted well into crop rotations.

The monastic farms also raised animals. Cattle were useful for milk, for pulling implements such as ploughs and as sources of hides. Sheep produced profitable wool and could also be milked. Some of the monastic flocks were quite large. The Cistercians' flocks ran into the thousands. Rievaulx had 14,000 sheep in the late 13th century. But the larger Benedictine houses were also experienced sheep farmers. By the time of the Domesday survey, for example, Ely had a flock of some 9,000 sheep.

The wool from these sheep was exported in large quantities, bringing in a considerable income. The Cistercians sold the most. A list from the late 13th century indicated that the white monks were exporting around 1,468 sacks of wool, while the Benedictines and Augustinians managed 460 and 424 sacks respectively. Each sack contained around 200 fleeces, so this was a sizeable trade.

All this activity made a huge impact on the landscape, with large areas enclosed for animals together with all the open-field arable farming. And the monasteries were famous for pushing at the boundaries of cultivable land, bringing areas into use that previous generations had regarded as waste.

Forests were a special target of monastic activity. Communities of monks or nuns needed forests for building timber and fuel. One popular way of exploiting woods was coppicing, cutting trees regularly to ground level. This produced small branches that were easy to cut and could be used in a variety of ways – as fence posts, firewood and for wattling, the basket-like weave of twigs used with daub to form the infill panels in timber-framed walls.

But coppicing did not produce the big timbers that were used to build roofs and other large structures. This was an issue for monasteries, because a large abbey included several big structures – a typical church, refectory, dormitory and infirmary hall were all broad buildings that needed substantial roof trusses. So many monasteries combined coppicing with growing full-size trees, sometimes mixing the two in the same wood. That way, they had enough timber ready when buildings were damaged by fire or when expansion plans led to larger buildings.

Coppicing was a highly efficient way of producing wood. Whereas oak trees had to grow for many decades to produce good-sized timber for building, an area of coppice could be cut much more frequently to produce tons of firewood, posts and other timber. By dividing up a wood and cutting a section at a time, there would always be some trees ready to cut and an abbey with large holdings could expect to have a surplus for sale.

Areas of forest could also be used for farming – for example pigs enjoy rooting around in oak forests. But if a monastery had more than enough woodland for timber and pigs a common solution was assarting – clearing areas of woodland for farming. This must have brought huge areas under the plough, transforming the landscape in the process.

Still more dramatic was the monastic exploitation of wetlands. To outsiders, these areas were often regarded as little more than useless. But locals knew that marshland could be a rich source of fish and waterfowl and could provide lush pasture in the drier summer periods. The monks exploited such lands, often also seizing the opportunity to cut reeds for thatch and to take turf for fuel. This was a valuable resource and more than one abbey got into a dispute with neighbours about the right to cut turves on abbey land.

But marshland could be even more valuable if it was drained and reclaimed, and this activity was pursued by a number of abbeys. The fringes of the Fens, home to many monasteries, were the scenes of this kind of activity. The first monks and nuns at abbeys such as Ely, Ramsey, Peterborough and Croyland were no doubt attracted to the area because it was remote. In these eastern marshes they must have felt at one remove from the world. But once the monks were settled there, the opportunities offered by the Fens were attractive. Even unimproved, they offered areas of good summer pasture. But with better drainage and the building of new granges, the land steadily became more productive.

There were similar developments in the moors of Somerset where Glastonbury Abbey held much land, on Romney Marsh amongst the lands of the cathedral-priory of Canterbury, on Barking Abbey's extensive lands on the Essex marshes and elsewhere. The medieval monks, who had retreated to the 'desert', often could not resist the temptation to improve their spartan environment and make it more productive.

In such areas the monasteries could transform the landscape. And even where there were no woods or marshes to reclaim, they could make a huge difference. For example there was a decline in arable farming in the late Middle Ages. Some monasteries did away with some of their large open fields, enclosing them to provide pasture for livestock.

Monastic fishponds, sometimes several per house, were another type of structure that made an impact on the landscape. These ponds, which were used for keeping fish caught in nearby lakes and rivers or donated

to the monks or nuns by patrons, were usually fed with water via channels from a local stream. They became common from the mid-12th century onwards and all sorts of freshwater fish were kept in them, including eels, tench, bream, pike and, sometimes, carp. The ponds varied in size. A few monasteries had huge ponds (occasionally up to 50 acres (20 hectares)), in which large numbers of fish could breed. But more common were smaller ponds in groups of three, four or more. Small ponds were usually interconnected with channels and sluice gates that could be closed, allowing individual ponds to be emptied and cleaned. Today, most ponds exist as earthworks, depressions in the ground that can often be seen clearly in aerial photographs. In a few places ponds survive filled with water – at Evesham, for example, two of the abbey's three fishponds are still filled.

It can be difficult to appreciate the effects of the monasteries on the landscape today because almost 500 years of further agricultural developments have followed the dissolution of the monasteries. Many of

The priory fishpond at Mount Grace is in front of the former guest house.

the buildings produced by this agriculture have also vanished. Substantial structures such as barns have survived in large numbers because they were big, stone-built and suitable for use by the farmers who carried on in place of the monks. But few other medieval farm buildings remain. The main reason for this is probably that they were built of wood so even where farming continued they eventually wore out and were replaced.

Thus hundreds of monastic cattle sheds, cart sheds, pigsties and similar buildings and features have disappeared, traceable only where their bases or foundations remain as earthworks. The same goes for granaries, of which there must have been hundreds. These were important buildings, for an abbey's store of grain was a lifeline, the basic raw material of both bread and beer. A granary had to be rodent proof and so was often raised off the ground (either on posts or on mushroom-shaped staddle stones), but it also needed to be well ventilated. One monastic granary does survive mainly intact – the one on the farm of Shaftesbury Abbey at Bradford-on-Avon. Even it has probably been much altered – the upper walls, now stone, were likely to have been timber-framed at one time.

The remains of domestic buildings on these outlying properties or granges survive more frequently because many became private houses at the dissolution. These buildings were where the steward or reeve – the official who looked after the abbey's lands – lived and they were designed like medieval manor houses; some orders even called them manors. They were centred around a hall, where the household ate and slept and this large room was linked to one or more private apartments at one end and at the other end to a service wing containing a pantry (food store) and buttery (the place where the butts of beer or wine were kept). There was also a kitchen near the pantry and buttery, but this was often in a detached building.

Some of the most impressive of these houses were built by the Benedictine monks and Augustinian canons. Their halls are frequently spacious, often with aisles in eastern England or with a cruck frame in the west. These are usually tall, double-height rooms, but in some places the old Norman arrangement of a first-floor hall above a ground-floor storage undercroft was favoured. Either way they can be sizeable structures where the steward could live almost as comfortably as the lord of a small manor. The Cistercians built similar houses, but on the whole on a smaller scale and with more basic facilities.

Most granges were built near a well or spring – they did not usually have the elaborate water supply arrangements of their parent monasteries and their sites were determined to give convenient access to the fields. Only a few had more sophisticated plumbing, like Malham, a grange of Fountains Abbey, which had lead water pipes by 1257.

Some monastic granges had a chapel for communal worship or an oratory, a smaller room for private prayer. On the whole monasteries resisted the temptation to build chapels – after all for regular worship there would usually be a parish church within striking distance of the grange or manor and the orders did not want to make a grange too much like home to visiting brothers. At one point the Cistercian general chapter even ruled against setting up altars in granges. But they had to relent when it became clear that the physical distances between grange and main abbey or church were sometimes too far for people to make the journey for regular worship. As so often in the history of the monasteries, a compromise had to be reached because of the conflict between ideals and geographical realities. A few of these grange chapels still stand, but most of them have been converted to other uses.

The monasteries and the villages

The rural impact of the monasteries went beyond the manor. The monks probably took part in the creation of new planned villages in the early Middle Ages, when agriculture was expanding. But they were also responsible for destroying villages and depopulating areas of the countryside.

The Cistercians in particular were well known for their effect on rural communities. Ideally, a Cistercian house was sited well away from other human habitations, so that its monks could isolate themselves from the concerns of the world. But often they were given land that was already partly settled. In such cases they were not above forcing the locals to move out. Earthworks marking the sites of the buildings and fields of deserted medieval villages can be found on many former Cistcerian estates as a result. There were 20 such villages on the lands of Fountains Abbey alone.

Many of these developments took place in the 12th century, when the reforming orders – including the Cistercians – were establishing themselves in Britain. Further changes came later in the Middle Ages. In the mid-14th century, for example, the Black Death struck, a plague that wiped out a huge proportion – probably between one-third and one-half – of the entire population. The bottom dropped out of the market for corn and many monasteries turned increasingly to livestock farming. This meant enclosing open fields, which could lead to friction with tenants who had survived the plague and were trying to hang on to common rights in land that an abbey wanted to fence off.

So depopulations continued alongside these enclosures and they posed enough of a problem for Parliament to pass a number of laws, starting in 1489, to try to stop them. Even then the practice continued and a commission of inquiry, set up by Cardinal Wolsey in the early 16th century, reported that some 40 monasteries had evicted tenants and demolished their houses. But the traffic was not all one way. Some monasteries actually put tenants back if it suited them to do so. In the 14th century, for example, a number of northern Cistercian abbeys reinstated tenants to farm some of their lands, a move designed to increase income from farming after a time of difficulty caused by damage in the wake of wars between England and Scotland. The impact of the monasteries on the countryside was varied, but it was nearly always significant.

The monasteries and the towns

Many monasteries were based in towns and therefore they also had a huge influence there. This is especially true of the Benedictines, many of whose houses were sited in towns. The Augustinian canons also held a lot of urban property and, of all the orders, the various groups of friars were the most urban of all.

Though some abbeys were founded in existing towns, it was not unusual for a town to form around an abbey. Monasteries were often sizeable communities. They aimed to be self-sufficient but in practice would have needed the services of all sorts of craft workers and traders. Many abbeys were also pilgrimage centres, attracting lots of visitors. From the point of view of a trader or an artisan, a base near an abbey was an attractive proposition.

A town could also be attractive to an abbey if it belonged to an order that looked favourably on the earning of income from rents. Thus sizeable settlements grew up around many abbeys, especially some of the larger Benedictine ones founded before the Norman conquest, such as Glastonbury, Evesham and Peterborough. After the conquest the trend continued, with towns growing up around abbeys such as Battle and other towns expanding as the neighbouring abbey grew – Bury St Edmunds is an example of this pattern.

Monasteries could also form towns on their outlying estates, often building on an existing settlement – where there might already have been a few farmers and some informal trading – in order to add rented houses with plots of land together with a market. The Cotswold town of Moreton-in-Marsh, for example, was a town created under the auspices of Westminster Abbey.

The long main street at Moreton-in-Marsh is the legacy of a 13th-century town-building project by Westminster Abbey.

The degree of monastic activity and influence in towns varied enormously. Many abbeys held urban property that they rented out to provide an income. There were scores of monastic properties in London (according to one estimate, around two-thirds of the capital was held by various church landlords); the ports of the east coast were also popular, because many monasteries were involved in the wool trade with Europe; and many other towns and cities included at least one religious house amongst their property holders.

Many monastic properties were inns, which fitted in with the abbeys' interest in pilgrimage (*see* pp 89–94). Some buildings, also known as inns, were more like large town houses. They could be used by the abbot on his travels and their outbuildings could be used to store goods that the monastery was trading. Some monasteries owned shops, which they rented out to tenants. A famous row of timber-framed medieval shops, still standing near Tewkesbury Abbey, was almost certainly built by the monks to generate an income.

The building and renting of shops was a natural extension of another monastic enterprise: the running of fairs and markets. More than 300 of the regular markets held in England in the Middle Ages belonged to monasteries and they traded in all sorts of commodities, from livestock to manufactured goods. Many of these markets started before the Norman conquest and were located outside the gates of abbeys. These early markets often had a wedge-shaped plan, which can still be seen next to former abbey precincts in places such as St Albans and Peterborough. Rectangular-shaped market places, by contrast, often indicate that the market was a later development, part of a piece of medieval town-planning based on a grid of streets.

A row of timber-framed shops near Tewkesbury Abbey was probably built by the monastery as a way of generating income.

Fairs, which were held once a year, were set up in many towns, often for the sale of one specific product, such as geese or wool. Like markets, many were founded and controlled by monasteries. If successful, they could attract merchants from all over the country or even overseas, and stalls would be set up all over the town. Occasionally a memory of a medieval fair survives in the name of a street name, such as London's Cloth Fair, which commemorates the famous Bartholomew Fair held next to St Bartholomew's Priory.

Towns are dynamic places and most have changed radically since the time of the dissolution. Thus tracing the monastic impact on town structure and layout is a specialised field, involving the detailed study of documents and plans. But there are still traces of the monastic influence on the ground, in the formal, linear plans of planned monastic towns like Moreton-in-Marsh, in areas where new medieval building produced grids of streets as in Bury St Edmunds and in places with less formal market areas that appeared outside abbey gates in the early Middle Ages.

The monasteries and parish churches

Many medieval monks were ordained priests but, since the reforms of the 10th century, they did not normally have the duties of a parish priest. The monk could and did pray for the lay population, but as a rule he did not administer the sacraments to lay people. But after the Norman conquest, a system was introduced that gave monasteries control over many parish churches. A monastery would be given a church, which gave it the right to a share of that church's income in return for appointing a parish priest. A hundred years after the conquest, probably about one quarter of all parish churches were controlled by monasteries in this way.

The way this system worked in practice varied, but often the monastery took over the entire income – all the tithes, in the form of corn, hay, timber, livestock and dairy produce, that the lay population regularly paid to the church. Some of the income was used to pay the vicar, the rest was taken by the monks. Alternatively, the abbey could keep the so-called 'great tithes' (grain, hay and timber), while the vicar was allotted the 'small tithes' (livestock, eggs and milk).

A monastery was responsible for repairs to the parish churches it owned. In theory, and in canon law, these repairs were supposed to cover the whole building, but in practice, the lay people usually cared for the nave while the abbey looked after the chancel. In the 13th century, when there was a new emphasis on the importance of the Mass (*see* pp 80–1), many monasteries improved the east ends of the churches in their possession. Occasionally, an entire church was rebuilt. Uffington in Berkshire, a church owned by Abingdon Abbey and extensively rebuilt in the mid-13th century, is a good example; however, rebuilding on this scale was costly and rare. Occasionally, a monastery would make other additions to churches under its control, building a chapel or an aisle,

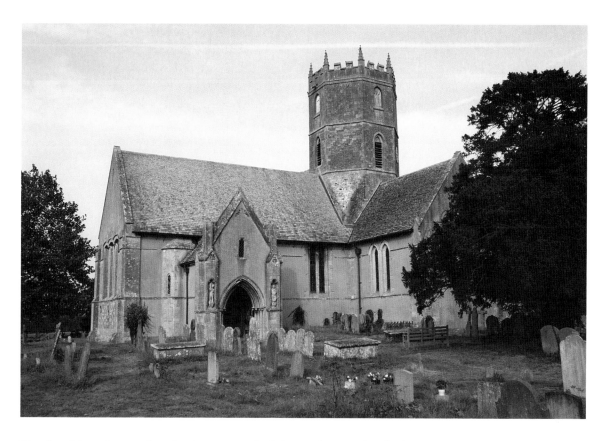

The parish church at Uffington belonged to Abingdon Abbey and was rebuilt in the 13th century.

like the aisle at Meare church, Somerset, which bears the initials of John Selwood, abbot of the controlling abbey of Glastonbury.

Many monastic churches were in the countryside, where there were rich tithes to be collected. But monasteries also had churches in towns. There were often religious reasons for this. In the urban areas where many Benedictine monasteries were found it was often difficult for monks to be as isolated from the world as they ideally wished. Traditionally, local people had worshipped in monastic naves, but this brought monastic and lay populations still closer together. Sometimes a separate parish church was built so that the lay people could worship separately. It did not have to be far from the monastery – one only has to look at the church of St Margaret's, Westminster, hard by the walls of Westminster Abbey, to appreciate this. But it was a separate space, giving the monks the isolation that was all too elusive in a great city. Many great urban abbeys, from Glastonbury to St Albans, built parish churches in their towns.

Gazetteer

AT THE TIME OF THE DISSOLUTION there were more than 1,000 monasteries in England and Wales, including some 200 friaries and over 130 nunneries. This gazetteer is a listing of around 290 of the most interesting. They include ruined sites and places where one or more specific buildings – for example a church or a gatehouse – have been preserved. The listing includes the majority of sites with substantial above-ground remains in England and Wales, together with a representative sample of sites where there are scant but interesting traces.

Each entry gives the name of the monastery, its county, its date of foundation (and refoundation where there are two or more dates) and its order. The designations EH, Cadw or NT indicate that the site is in the care of English Heritage, Cadw or the National Trust. Sites in the care of these heritage bodies are normally open to the public (relevant web sites give opening times).

Many other sites, including the monastic cathedrals and many parish churches, are also open. Other sites are privately owned and access may be restricted, though remains can often be seen from public roads or footpaths.

The interior of the church at Hexham was built in the Early English style.

Abbotsbury Abbey
Dorset 1026/1044 Benedictine monks EH

A few fragments of wall, the gable end of a cloister building, the remains of two gatehouses, a dovecote and a barn are the main survivals from this Benedictine house. The most impressive building is the barn, one of the best in England. Half of this great structure, which was originally over 270ft (82m) in length, is intact and roofed.

Abingdon Abbey
Oxfordshire 675/954 Benedictine monks

Abingdon was refounded in 954 after destruction by the Danes. Under its abbot, Aethelwold, it became one of the most important centres of the 10th-century renewal of monasticism. The church has vanished and there are only scant remains of the rest of the buildings. These include a late 15th-century gateway and a range of buildings along the river including the Long Gallery of c 1500 and the 13th-century checker (or office), which has a fine, gable-topped chimney stack.

Alnwick Abbey
Northumberland 1148 Premonstratensian canons

The strong-looking 14th-century gatehouse is the last remnant of Alnwick Abbey, standing among the parkland of the great Alnwick Castle.

Barking Abbey
Essex 666/c 965 Benedictine nuns and monks

Founded by St Erkenwald, bishop of London, and refounded after attacks by the Danes, Barking Abbey was once one of the most important Benedictine nunneries. The buildings have largely vanished, but the site has been excavated and the plan can be seen picked out on the grass. The one standing building is the eastern or Fire Bell Gate, which is of two storeys with battlements.

Barnwell Priory
Cambridgeshire 1092 Augustinian canons

A small 13th-century church in Cambridge's Newmarket Road was probably the gate chapel of Barnwell Priory. It is a simple building with just a nave and chancel under a single roof and a 20th-century porch.

Basingwerk Abbey
Clwyd 1131 Savigniac/Cistercian monks Cadw

This Savigniac foundation was absorbed by the Cistercian order. Amongst the ruins, which show much evidence of major rebuilding in the early 13th century, the chapter house and monks' refectory are easiest to make out.

Bath Abbey
Avon/North Somerset 676/758/1090 Benedictine nuns/monks

Bath Abbey began in 676 as a nunnery. The nuns were replaced by monks in 758 and the house was refounded in 1090 after it was destroyed by the Danes. By the end of the 15th century the abbey's buildings were in disrepair and a magnificent new church was begun. This is one of the finest examples of English late medieval architecture, with tall arches, big windows and stunning fan vaults. At the dissolution the abbey was offered to the city, but the price of 500 marks (£333) proved too high and the property went to a private owner. But in 1560 the owner, Edmund Colthurst, gave the church to the town and it has remained in use for worship to this day. The nave had a timber roof until the 19th century, but the fine fan vault that matches the one in the choir was completed by 1869.

Battle Abbey
East Sussex 1067 Benedictine monks EH

After the Norman conquest, King William founded Battle Abbey in atonement for the deaths during the fighting. The altar of the church was said to be placed at the very place where Harold, the English king, met his death. Many of the buildings were converted to a house at the dissolution. The imposing 14th-century gatehouse can still be seen and there are ruined cloister buildings, including the dormitory, which survives as a roofless shell.

The vaulted novices' room at Battle Abbey is at the southern end of the dormitory range.

Bayham Abbey

Kent 1208 Premonstratensian canons EH

High walls of the transepts of the church survive at Bayham, together with the eastern cloister range. The crossing piers, with their clusters of shafts, and the pointed arches in the transepts give some idea of the pure Early English Gothic style of the building. Carvings of foliage show the quality of the stonework.

Beaulieu Abbey

Hampshire 1203/1204 Cistercian monks

The abbey of Beaulieu was founded by King John and was one of the largest Cistercian abbeys in England, centred on a church 336ft (102m) long. Today, this great church survives only as an outline on the ground, together with the south wall of the nave where it adjoins the cloister. The chapter house entrance, with its three arches, can be seen, as can the

grand doorway that connected the eastern walk with the church. There are two important domestic buildings still standing and roofed – the cloister's western range and the monks' refectory, which was converted to the parish church at the dissolution. Inside the original reader's pulpit and its stairway are preserved. The abbey is now in the grounds of the National Motor Museum.

Beauvale Charterhouse

Nottinghamshire 1320 Carthusian monks

Fragments of the Carthusian monastery survive abutting on to a later farm.

Beeleigh Abbey

Essex c 1180 Premonstratensian canons

The 13th-century chapter house with Purbeck marble piers and the undercroft of the dormitory survive, together with buildings incorporated into a 16th-century house.

Beeston Regis Priory

Norfolk c 1216 Augustinian canons

Substantial remains of the church of this small coastal priory can be seen. The building had an aisleless nave, a chancel and a north transept. Flint was the main building material, as was usual in this part of East Anglia.

Beverley Blackfriars

East Riding of Yorkshire c 1240 Dominican friars

Stone, brick and timber buildings belonging to the Dominican friary

have been restored for use as a youth hostel.

Bicknacre Priory

Essex 1175 Augustinian canons

One crossing arch in a field is all that survives of the 13th-century church of Bicknacre Priory.

Bilsington Priory

Kent 1253 Augustinian canons

A domestic building, probably the infirmary, survives from this small Augustinian house on ground overlooking Romney Marsh. The building was rather heavily restored in the early 20th century.

Bindon Abbey

Dorset 1171/1172 Cistercian monks

Monks from Forde Abbey first settled on a site near Lulworth Cove before quickly moving to a more sheltered location near the village of Wool. The founder, Roger de Newburgh, gave the abbey substantial lands, together with the right to hold a weekly market and annual fair at Wool. The low walls of their church and parts of the eastern cloister range survive.

Binham Priory

Norfolk 1091 Benedictine monks EH

Seven 12th-century bays of the monastic church survive in parochial use. The ruins of the crossing together with various domestic remains – mostly very low flint walls – can be seen south of the church.

The entrance and chapel preserve part of the structure of the former Templar building at Bisham Abbey.

Bisham Abbey

Berkshire 1337/1537 Knights Templar/
Augustinian canons/Benedictine monks

Parts of the Templars' building survive in the structure of the house built by the Hoby family after the dissolution.

Blanchland Abbey

Northumberland 1165 Premonstratensian canons

The parish church at Blanchland consists of the transept and chancel of the monastic church. Many of the buildings in the village are converted or reused parts of the monastery – for example a tower was probably the abbot's lodging.

Blyth Priory

Nottinghamshire 1088 Benedictine monks

The only surviving part of the priory is the western part of the church. This is largely early Norman, with round arches and very little decoration.

Bolton Priory

North Yorkshire 1120/1154–5 Augustinian canons

The early 14th-century east end of the church (chancel and transepts) stands as substantial ruins, while the earlier nave is in parochial use. The 16th-century west tower still stands, acting as an entrance to the nave. Foundations of the cloister buildings also survive.

Bordesley Abbey

Worcestershire 1138 Cistercian monks

Most of the substantial stone buildings here were demolished soon after the dissolution, but were then left undisturbed until they were first excavated in the 19th century. This excavation revealed many foundations buried underground; a series of further excavations in the late 20th century investigated their often complex history. There were many changes at Bordesley, partly because of alterations in liturgy, partly because of the difficult site: a wet valley bottom. Low wall remains and foundations – mainly of the church – together with earthworks of the cloister and remains of a water mill can be seen in the setting of a public park.

Boston Blackfriars

Lincolnshire c 1280 Dominican friars

Boston's Blackfriars' Hall was probably the refectory of the Dominican friary. This 13th- or 14th-century building is all that remains of the town's four medieval friaries.

Bourne Priory

Lincolnshire 1138 Augustinian canons

When the Augustinian priory at Bourne was dissolved, the community kept part of the church for their own use and this is all that remains of the monastic buildings. There are four bays of the Norman nave, with round piers. The chancel was rebuilt in the 19th century.

The guest house is one of the more substantial remains at Boxgrove Priory.

Boxgrove Priory
West Sussex 1105 Benedictine monks EH

At the dissolution, the locals retained the east end of the priory church for their own use. The chancel is a superb example of early Gothic architecture, with pointed arches, lancet windows and fine stone vaulting. A few fragments of the other buildings remain, including a chapter house doorway.

Boxley Abbey
Kent 1143/1146 Cistercian monks

Fragmentary remains of this Cistercian abbey survive amongst the landscape gardens of a private house north of Maidstone. To the south-west is a 13th-century abbey barn almost 185ft (56m) in length.

Bradford-on-Avon tithe barn
Wiltshire 14th century (abbey foundation 888) Benedictine nuns EH

This magnificent tithe barn was part of a grange of Shaftesbury Abbey. Its stone walls and wooden roof make it one of the most impressive monastic barns and there are generous doorways that allowed carts to be driven right inside.

Bradwell Priory
Buckinghamshire 1136 Benedictine monks

Little remains of this small Benedictine house except for some fragments – two 14th-century doorways and some windows – in a building belonging to Abbey Farm near the parish church.

Brecon Priory (now Cathedral)
Powys 1110 Benedictine monks

The priory church became a cathedral in 1923. Much of the fabric dates from the 13th and 14th centuries; highlights include the elegant 13th-century chancel, vaulted in the 19th century. The precinct wall is pierced by two gateways.

Brinkburn Priory
Northumberland 1135 Augustinian canons EH

The church was built towards the end of the 12th century and shows the transition from Norman architecture, with its round arches, to Gothic, with its pointed openings. A Norman doorway and groups of lancet windows are among the architectural pleasures. There are also fragments of the cloister, but most of the domestic buildings were absorbed into the neighbouring mansion.

The canons' church at Brinkburn is in a beautiful plain early Gothic style, with rows of lancet windows.

Bristol Abbey (now Cathedral)
Bristol 1140 Augustinian canons

The chapter house, sumptuously carved inside, is the most striking survival from the early phase of the Augustinian house at Bristol. Their church, which was made into a cathedral by Henry VIII, was remodelled in a building campaign that began in 1298 and the choir and eastern Lady Chapel date from this period. This is stunning work, with beautiful vaults, arches and other details. The nave was being rebuilt at the dissolution and its low walls were demolished. The cathedral did without a nave until G E Street was commissioned to design a new one, built between 1867 and 1877.

Bristol Blackfriars
Bristol 1227–8 Dominican friars

A number of buildings around a courtyard have their origins in the friary set up in Bristol in the 1220s. One, known from later occupants as Cutlers' Hall, was probably the dormitory. Another, Bakers' Hall, is likely to have been the infirmary; it has a timber-framed roof, probably from the 14th century.

Bromfield Priory
Shropshire 1155 Benedictine monks

The monks' nave survives as the parish church and preserves details from various dates in the Middle Ages. The other survival is the 14th-century gatehouse, a long structure with a massively buttressed lower storey and timber framing above.

Broomholm Priory
Norfolk 1113/1195 Cluniac monks

A ruined gatehouse leads to the remains of the priory church – including a Norman transept – and traces of the cloister buildings. Broomholm was important in the Middle Ages because it possessed a relic of the True Cross and, as a result, was a destination for pilgrims from all over the country.

Buckfast Abbey
Devon 1018/1136
Benedictine/Savigniac/Cistercian monks

There had been a Benedictine abbey on this site since before the Norman conquest, but by the 12th century it was probably in decline. In 1136 King Stephen, a supporter of the Savigniacs, stepped in and granted its possessions to the abbey of Savigny. Thus Buckfast became a Savigniac house until this group became part of the Cistercian order in 1147. After the dissolution, the buildings were left to decay until a Gothic-style house was built on the site in the first decade of the 19th century. This was bought in 1882 by a group of Benedictine monks from La Pierre-qui-Vire in France and the site has been a Benedictine monastery ever since. The Benedictine community rebuilt the abbey church on the medieval foundations. Excavations have revealed remains of a large 14th-century guest hall to the west of the church.

Buckland Abbey
Devon 1278 Cistercian monks NT

The Grenville family converted this Cistercian abbey into a house after the dissolution, taking the unusual step of adapting the church itself rather than some of the domestic buildings. The transepts were removed but most of the structure of the nave and choir remains, together with the low tower between them. The building became famous later in the 16th century as the home of Sir Francis Drake. In spite of various alterations and restorations, including one after a fire in 1938, much of the church structure survives. There is little left of the cloister buildings, but there is a fine great barn of the 14th or 15th century, which is approximately 160ft (49m) long with an arch-braced timber roof. Another notable precinct building, originally a stable, also survives.

Buildwas Abbey
Shropshire 1135 Savigniac/Cistercian monks EH

Much of the 12th-century church remains as a noble ruin, with many of the walls standing almost to roof level – because of this Buildwas is one of the best places to get an idea of the simplicity of an early Cistercian church. The nave piers are simple and round, supporting equally plain arches – the only decoration is the scalloped carving around the capitals. Above is a clerestory with equally unadorned,

The chapter house is just one of the fine medieval structures remaining at Buildwas Abbey.

round-headed windows. The square-ended chancel, slightly later, is similarly plain. The monks put their cloister buildings to the north of the church, where they could make use of the nearby River Severn for drainage. There are substantial remains here, including a superb chapter house, its rib-vaulted interior supported on four tall piers – two round and two octagonal. There is a groin-vaulted crypt below. The library-cum-sacristy, parlour and dormitory undercroft are also along the eastern range and the basement of the western cloister range also survives.

Burnham Norton Priory
Norfolk *c* 1241 Carmelite friars

The gatehouse of this small Carmelite friary is an example of flushwork masonry, a way of making patterns with a mixture of flint and dressed stone that was

popular in East Anglia in the Middle Ages. This is all that remains except for a few fragments of wall from the friary church.

Bury St Edmunds Abbey
Suffolk 633/1020 Benedictine monks EH

The precinct of this once-great abbey is now a public park and cemetery, and the low walls of the abbey buildings can still be seen. The chief surviving glories are the abbey's two gatehouses. The earlier of the two is a tall Norman tower, which acted both as a gateway to the abbey and the belfry of St James's church. The other is shorter and in elegant 14th-century Gothic style.

Bushmead Priory
Bedfordshire 1195 Augustinian canons EH

The 13th-century refectory – with its original timber-framed roof and some wall paintings – is the main survival of this small Augustinian

house. At the dissolution the building was divided horizontally and new windows were inserted upstairs. These retain some of their old glass.

Butley Priory
Suffolk 1171 Augustinian canons

Excavations revealed the plan of the church, of which an arch of *c* 1300 remains; farm buildings absorbed some of the adjacent structures, such as the refectory and dormitory. But the stunning survivor is the gatehouse, added in the 1320s and lavishly decorated with flushwork masonry, Gothic tracery and heraldic panels.

Byland Abbey
North Yorkshire 1134/1177 Savigniac/Cistercian monks EH

Byland was the final site chosen by a group of monks who had tried from 1134 onwards to colonise other northern sites that had proved unsuitable. The remains at Byland have been extensively excavated and many low walls and foundations reveal the plan of the buildings. A fragment of the south transept stands quite high, revealing the fine stonework of the details of the arches and windows. But the glory of Byland is the ruined west front of the church. There are round-headed and Gothic entrance doorways at ground level, elegant pointed lancet windows and blind arches above and, higher still, the remains of a large rose window.

Calder Abbey

Cumbria 1134/1142 Savigniac/Cistercian monks

This small abbey was never prosperous and seems to have had only a handful of monks for most of its life. There are quite extensive remains of the church, which has a round-headed doorway of the 1170s and much 13th-century fabric. Parts of the eastern cloister range remain – notably of the chapter house and dormitory – while the southern range was absorbed into an 18th-century house.

Canons Ashby Priory

Northamptonshire 1151 Augustinian canons

A small part of the grand monastic church survives in parochial use. It consists of two bays of the 13th-century nave with its north aisle. There is also a tower, built in the mid-14th century. The domestic buildings have long vanished, but there is a small well house in a nearby field.

Canonsleigh Abbey

Devon 1161/1285 Augustinian canonesses

Originally founded for Augustinian canons, this house was transferred to the canonesses in 1285. The main survival is the gatehouse, now found amongst later farm buildings.

Canterbury Blackfriars

Kent 1237 Dominican friars

The flint-fronted refectory – a 13th-century building standing above a vaulted undercroft – is all that survives of Canterbury's Dominican friary.

Canterbury Cathedral Priory

Kent 997 Benedictine monks

The Saxon monastery on this site was refounded in the 10th century. Soon after the Norman conquest a major rebuilding campaign began, but much of the east end dates from just over a century later, when the church was remodelled after a fire and in response to the murder of Archbishop Thomas Becket in 1170. A shrine was created for Becket's remains and a new east end in the Gothic style constructed. Canterbury, already the headquarters of the church in England, became a major place of pilgrimage. The western portion of the church was rebuilt in the Perpendicular style later in the Middle Ages. Lots of domestic buildings also remain, including the early dormitory and the infirmary, together with the chapter house and the fine early 16th-century Christ Church Gate.

Cardiff Blackfriars

Cardiff Late 13th century Dominican friars

In the park next to Cardiff Castle are the foundations of the city's Dominican friary. The remains were excavated in the time of John Patrick Stuart, 3rd Marquis of Bute, who commissioned the architect William Burges to recreate the castle.

Carlisle Cathedral Priory

Cumbria 1122 Augustinian canons

Carlisle was a cathedral-priory that kept its cathedral status at the dissolution. The church, though oddly proportioned (the eastern arm is wider than the nave), has some beautiful details. There are Norman arches in the nave and the chancel is a noble space of 1220–50, with a magnificent east window of the early 14th century. The capitals in the chancel are finely carved with foliage and activities representing the months of the year. The refectory (now a library), with its reading pulpit and vaulted undercroft, is the best survival from the domestic buildings of the priory.

Carrow Priory

Norfolk 1146 Benedictine nuns

The prioress's house – Carrow was strictly a priory not an abbey – is the main survivor. It was bought by Jeremiah Colman of the mustard company in 1878 and has remained in the company's hands ever since.

Cartmel Priory

Cumbria 1194 Augustinian canons

The church, with its crossing tower topped with a lantern, contains 15th-century stalls with misericords. The building survives as the parish church.

Castle Acre Priory

Norfolk 1089 Cluniac monks EH

These are probably the most impressive of England's Cluniac

ruins. The main surviving part of the church is the west front, which is a major piece of Norman design featuring blind arcading and three doorways; there is also a later window. There is plenty of interest amongst the cloister ruins too, including the chapter house, dormitory undercroft and a large reredorter. The western range has an outstanding prior's residence of around 1500, as showy and large as a manor house.

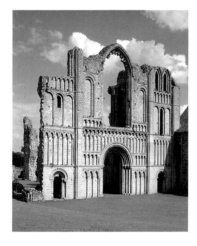

The west front at Castle Acre is a typically ornate piece of Cluniac design.

Cerne Abbey
Dorset 987 Benedictine monks

Various fragments of the medieval buildings of this Benedictine monastery survive at Abbey House – the abbey gatehouse, the highly decorative porch to the abbot's lodgings and a plainer two-storey building said to be the guest house. There is also a small barn nearby.

Chester Abbey (now Cathedral)
Cheshire 1093 Benedictine monks

The Benedictine abbey of Chester became a cathedral in 1541 after the dissolution. The medieval church was repeatedly restored in the 19th century, but Norman work survives in the north transept and north-west tower, and an east end of the 13th and early 14th centuries and a later medieval nave can also be seen. The cloister and its buildings are very interesting. There is a beautifully vaulted chapter house, a warming room with two fireplaces and a refectory that still has its reading pulpit and stairs. The nearby Abbey Square and Abbey Street were originally part of the precinct and the abbey gatehouse is in one corner of the square.

Christchurch Priory
Dorset 1150 Augustinian canons

The church is the sole survivor of this important Augustinian house, but it is one of the most magnificent of all Norman churches. Intersecting arches, latticework and other forms of carved decoration adorn the exterior. Inside there are big Norman piers in the nave. The east end is later – from the 15th and 16th centuries – with big windows and lots of light.

The surviving walls of the nave at the Church of the Holy Sepulchre, Thetford, are built of flint rubble.

Church of the Holy Sepulchre, Thetford
Norfolk 1139 Canons of the Holy Sepulchre EH

On the western side of Thetford are the ruins of the nave of a church, originally the heart of a priory of the Canons of the Holy Sepulchre. These are the only traces in England of a house of this order.

Cirencester Abbey
Gloucestershire 1117 Augustinian canons

The Spital Gate, with its great Norman archway and smaller pedestrian entrance, is the only standing portion of this once-large Augustinian abbey.

Clare Priory

Suffolk 1248 Austin friars

This is properly a friary, not a priory, and was the first English house of the Austin friars. The western range of the cloister, converted first to the friary guest house and later to a private house, survives. The long church remains as an evocative ruin.

Cleeve Abbey

Somerset 1186/1198 Cistercian monks EH

The church at Cleeve has gone, but what sets this site apart is its collection of cloister buildings, the most complete of any English Cistercian abbey. One of the highlights is the refectory, a spacious 15th-century building with high three-light windows and a superb wooden arch-braced roof featuring carvings of angels. Another is the gatehouse, originally

Cleeve Abbey's gatehouse is a compact building adorned with a crucifix on its southern gable.

13th century. Much of the dormitory undercroft is also preserved and the dormitory itself still has its walls and lancet windows. In addition there are some remarkable smaller rooms, one of which has wall paintings that include a portrayal of St Catherine with her wheel. Little remains of the western cloister range, though the cloister walk itself – rebuilt shortly before the dissolution – is well preserved.

Clifford Priory

Herefordshire 1130 Cluniac monks

Little is left of Clifford Priory, isolated on the Welsh border in Herefordshire. A few details survive in the private house that now stands on the site.

Cockersand Abbey

Lancashire 1184/1190 Premonstratensian canons

The chapter house of the abbey is the sole remnant, surviving because it has been used as the mausoleum of the Dalton family of nearby Thurnham Hall. The building has a beautiful rib-vaulted interior of around 1230.

Coggeshall Abbey

Essex 1140 Savigniac/Cistercian monks

In 1140 King Stephen and Queen Matilda founded Coggeshall Abbey. Unusually, bricks were used in the construction; this makes the abbey one of the earliest post-Roman brick buildings in England with the exception of those in which old Roman bricks were reused. The southern end of the dormitory undercroft – dating from the late 12th century – is the main surviving structure, together with a free-standing building of similar date slightly to the south, which may have been a guest house. In addition there is the gatehouse chapel, with lancet windows, which is probably early 13th century. The remains are in the grounds of a private house.

Coombe Abbey

Warwickshire 1150 Cistercian monks

The cloister of this abbey was converted into a house at the dissolution and the church demolished. The house underwent several phases of rebuilding, but some medieval fragments can still be seen, including a round-headed chapter house doorway and 15th-century arches.

Cornworthy Abbey

Devon 1238 Augustinian nuns

The early 15th-century gatehouse of this nunnery is the main survival. It has two arches: one for pedestrians and one for wheeled traffic, both arched and vaulted.

Coventry Greyfriars

Warwickshire 1234 Franciscan friars

Only the spire, a mid-14th-century structure, survives from the church of the Franciscan friars in Coventry.

Coventry Whitefriars

Warwickshire 1342 Carmelite friars

Part of the quarters of this friary – the vaulted chapter house, dormitory and some cloister vaulting – survives, having been converted to a house and subsequently a museum.

Coverham Abbey

North Yorkshire 1202 Premonstratensian canons

Parts of the nave arcade and north transept of the church still stand on private land, visible from a public right of way. The guest house was incorporated into a later private Georgian house.

Coxford Priory

Norfolk c 1216 Augustinian canons

Minimal ruined walls of the canons' church survive next to earthworks marking the site of the domestic buildings.

Craswall Priory

Herefordshire c 1225 Grandmontine monks

A few fragments of wall mark the site of Craswall Priory, one of only three English houses of the order of Grandmont, an austere order inspired by the desert hermits, which was founded in France in the late 11th century.

Creake Abbey

Norfolk 1206 Augustinian canons EH

The ruins of the canons' church stand quite high in places, especially at the east end, where there are numerous complete 13th-century Gothic arches and window openings.

Croxden Abbey

Staffordshire 1176 Cistercian monks EH

Croxden was once a prosperous abbey that owed its wealth to sheep farming, but now the site is sadly bisected by a road that slices directly through the ruins of the church. Most of the visible remains are to the south-west of the road, comprising the west front and south wall of the church, parts of the south transept, the eastern cloister range, the infirmary and part of the abbot's lodgings. The west front has tall lancets and a doorway of four recessed orders in the style of the early 13th century.

Croyland Abbey

Lincolnshire 716/971 Benedictine monks

This ancient abbey was rebuilt several times. The present building – with one aisle surviving in parochial use and the rest of the church in ruins – dates from successive reconstructions after an earthquake in 1118 and a fire in 1143. The evocative ruins include much of the imposing west front but no cloister buildings survive.

Cwmhir Abbey

Powys 1176 Cistercian monks

The remains here are fragmentary: hidden but atmospheric. They consist mainly of the low walls of the very long nave, which was begun in the early 13th century.

The nave originally had 14 bays and was approximately 256ft (78m) in length, making this the largest monastic church in Wales, with space for a community of 60 monks. There are no remains of the cloister or its buildings.

Cymer Abbey

Gwynedd 1198 Cistercian monks Cadw

In a quiet setting near Dolgellau, some high walls, a Gothic arcade and a few lancet windows combine to give a good impression of the little monastic church at Cymer. A few fragments of the cloister buildings remain to the south and parts of the guest hall may be incorporated into a nearby farm.

Deerhurst Priory

Gloucestershire 9th century/1059 Benedictine monks

The church of the Saxon priory at Deerhurst became the parish church after the dissolution. Though it was much altered during the Middle Ages, it is still the best example of a Saxon monastic church that has survived. A tower, doorway, carvings, a font and numerous window openings (some blocked) survive from the pre-conquest period. An adjacent house incorporates some of the medieval domestic buildings.

Denny Abbey

Cambridgeshire 1159 Benedictine monks/
Knights Templar/Franciscan nuns EH

The monastery at Denny began
life as a Benedictine house,
founded from the cathedral-priory
at Ely. It did not thrive under the
Benedictines and was acquired by
the Templars in 1170. Some time
after the order of the Templars was
abolished in 1312 it was bought by
Mary de Valence, Countess of
Pembroke, who set up an abbey for
the nuns of St Clare. The nuns
built themselves a new church and
converted the old church for
domestic use. What remains on the
site today is the building that began
life as the west end of the old
church, its numerous blocked
openings showing how it evolved
over the years. There is also a
separate building – the nuns'
refectory – dating from the mid-
14th century.

Dieulacres Abbey

Staffordshire 1158/1214 Cistercian monks

Little remains of this foundation.
The main traces visible above
ground are earthworks, the bases of
early 13th-century crossing piers
and reused medieval stonework in
the farmhouse built on the site.

Dorchester Abbey

Oxfordshire 634/1140 Augustinian canons

This very early foundation was
refounded for the canons in 1140.
What remains is the magnificent
abbey church, which is partly 12th
century. However, its most

beautiful details are from a
remodelling in the 14th century,
when a new choir was built and
adorned with stunning sculpture,
including a window carved with
figures representing the Jesse Tree.

Dore Abbey

Herefordshire 1147 Cistercian monks

The monks at Dore began to build
a magnificent stone church – an
embellishment of the earlier
buildings on the site – in around
1175. Most of the domestic
buildings and the nave of the
church have gone, but what
remains is the entire east end of
the church, which is roofed, well
preserved and in use as the parish
church since it was restored by
Lord Scudamore in the 1630s. This
is a superb building, consisting of
tall transepts and choir, plus a
passage or ambulatory around the
choir, the latter beautifully vaulted
in stone. Lancet windows flanked
with shafts mirror the shafted piers
beneath. The building's contents
include fragments of masonry from
the rest of the abbey (for example
handsome carved roof bosses) and
some fine 17th-century woodwork.

Dover Priory

Kent 1136 Benedictine monks

Many of the buildings of the priory
are now part of Dover College, a
public school. They include the
guest house, now the school's
chapel, the fine Norman refectory,
now the school's hall, and the 14th-
century priory gatehouse.

Dunkeswell Abbey

Devon 1201 Cistercian monks

Only a few fragments remain of
this monastery, including some
medieval masonry incorporated
into the structure of the 19th-
century parish church, which was
built on the site of the abbey's
nave.

Dunstable Priory

Bedfordshire 1125 Augustinian canons

Apart from the outer gatehouse,
the main survival of this town-
centre priory is the nave of the
church, which was always used by
the parish and continued as the
parish church after the dissolution.
Much of the building is late 12th
century and Norman in style – the
grand Norman western portal with
its recessed orders also survives.
But in the 13th century the canons
built an impressive new west front
around this portal, with rows of
lancet-shaped niches in the now-
fashionable Gothic style. Later still,
in the 15th century, they added the
north-west tower.

Dunster Priory

Somerset 1090 Benedictine monks

Apart from a few Norman
fragments, the church – now in
parochial use – dates mainly from
the 15th and 16th centuries. The
crossing and tower date to the
1440s and the rest came in the
following decades. A few scattered
priory buildings also remain –
notably the prior's house, a round
dovecote and a 16th-century barn.

The nave of the cathedral-priory at Durham, with its boldly patterned piers, is one of the most important Norman structures in Britain.

Durham Cathedral Priory

County Durham 1083 Benedictine monks

Durham has been a major religious centre for over a thousand years. In 995 it became the home of the shrine of St Cuthbert, one of the most magnetic early Christian leaders in Britain. The cathedral church is one of the most important Norman buildings in the country and its setting next to the castle above the River Wear is second to none. Its interior, especially the nave with its massive piers, some incised with bold decorative patterns, is outstanding. Later additions include the western Galilee Chapel of *c* 1175 with its vistas of Norman arches, the Chapel of the Nine Altars at the east end in the Gothic style and the late medieval crossing tower. Adjoining the church is the cloister, which has many of its original buildings such as the chapter house, parlour and dormitory.

Duxford Chapel

Cambridgeshire Before 1286 Knights Hospitaller EH

This 13th-century chapel, consisting of nave and chancel, belonged to the Knights Hospitaller. The building was first mentioned in 1286.

Easbourne Priory

West Sussex *c* 1238 Augustinian canonesses

This house of Augustinian canonesses used the parish church for their worship. The remains of some of their domestic buildings are incorporated into the building that adjoins the church, where medieval details such as the arches of the chapter house entrance can still be picked out among the later work.

Easby Abbey

North Yorkshire 1155 Premonstratensian canons EH

There are ruins of the cloister buildings here and the refectory of *c* 1300 still has high walls above an undercroft. There is also a gatehouse of about the same date.

Ecclesfield Priory

West Yorkshire Early 12th century Benedictine monks

This was an alien priory, dependent on the abbey of St Wandrille in Normandy. It survives as a house called The Priory, which contains an early 14th-century chapel with an undercroft.

Egglestone Abbey

County Durham 1190s Premonstratensian canons EH

Parts of the church stand to a level above the tops of the windows, giving an idea of the solid-looking Norman nave, with some tiny round-headed windows, and the later chancel, with bigger 13th-century windows that would have let in plenty of light. The cloister survives only as foundations and fragments of walling, but the undercroft of the reredorter can also be seen.

Ellerton Priory

North Yorkshire 1189 Cistercian nuns

Little survives of the nuns' church except a late medieval west tower with a Norman arch leading into what was once the nave.

Elstow Abbey

Bedfordshire 1078 Benedictine nuns

The western section of the nunnery's nave was preserved as the parish church, to which an east end was added in 1580. The tall nave is a mixture of Norman and early Gothic work. To the south of the west front is a room that was once known as the chapter house but was probably the monastic outer parlour. Other fragments of the monastic buildings are concealed in the nearby Hillersdon Hall, which was built in 1616 using stone from the abbey.

Ely Cathedral Priory

Cambridgeshire 673/970 Benedictine nuns and monks

The priory was originally founded as a double house in 673 and was refounded for monks in 970. It became a cathedral-priory in 1109. By the end of the 12th century, the church was one of the country's most impressive buildings and the Norman nave still survives with its rows of round arches. In 1322 the Norman crossing tower collapsed and the decision was made to rebuild the crossing in a new form – a unique octagonal lantern. This glorious Gothic structure, made mostly of timber but imitating the

form of stone vaulting, creates one of the most beautiful spaces in all medieval architecture. The cloister buildings have largely gone, but a number of the precinct buildings, such as the guest house, prior's lodging and infirmary, still exist.

Evesham Abbey

Worcestershire 701/995 Benedictine monks

A stunning free-standing bell tower, finished just before the dissolution, is the main relic of the once large and rich abbey of Evesham. Its carved and panelled sides are a much-loved landmark in the town. The almonry – a building where alms were distributed (now a museum) – stands nearby.

Ewenny Priory

Mid Glamorgan 1141 Benedictine

The Norman nave is now used as the parish church. It has massive piers, as does its mother church, the abbey of St Peter in Gloucester. Nearby is a precinct wall with towers and gatehouses, showing that the place was once well defended.

Finchale Priory

County Durham 1196 Benedictine monks EH

This small priory was home to between 8 and 15 monks in the 13th century. By the following century it was used as a rest house for monks from Durham, who came in groups of four to join the resident prior. The change from

The ruins of the prior's hall at Finchale reveal a large room of manor-house scale.

priory to rest house meant that the buildings were altered – the church was shorn of its aisles and the refectory was abandoned because the monks ate at the prior's table. Even so, there are still substantial ruins here, including the walls and undercroft of the refectory and the prior's house, also with an undercroft. The walls of the church, including rows of round piers supporting arches that were filled in during the 14th century, still stand high.

Flanesford Priory

Herefordshire 1346 Augustinian canons

The refectory of this small priory survives as a private house. There are Decorated-style windows in stone walls beneath a pantile roof.

Flaxley Abbey

Gloucestershire 1151 Cistercian monks

Monks from Bordesley first came to Flaxley in 1151 when the abbey was founded by Earl Roger of Hereford. The site was said to be the place where Roger's father had died in a hunting accident. Today a country house stands on the site of the cloister. This house, not normally open to the public, incorporates parts of the medieval building such as part of one vaulted range of the cloister.

Forde Abbey

Dorset 1136/1141 Cistercian monks

A Cistercian foundation at Brightley in Devon failed (perhaps due to a difficult site and poor funding) and the monks relocated to Forde, by the River Axe in Dorset. Here they attracted further endowments and eventually flourished. Nothing remains of the church, but much of the cloister was used as the basis of a 17th-century house. Many of these rooms have been little altered since the creation of the house. Notable are the 13th-century dormitory and undercroft, together with the refectory, which was remodelled in the 15th century. The fine chapter house – a rectangular, rib-vaulted room – was converted to form a chapel for the house. The other important survivals are the lavish apartments of Thomas Chard, the last abbot of Forde.

The great tower at Fountains Abbey was one of the buildings created by Abbot Huby, who was head of the monastery from 1495 to 1526 – he left his mark on nearly every part of the abbey.

Fountains Abbey

North Yorkshire 1132 Cistercian monks
NT

In the early 12th century, a group of monks from St Mary's Abbey in York started a new house under the guidance of Archbishop Thurstan of York, settling in the valley of the River Skell near Ripon. They sought admission to the Cistercian order, acquired huge estates and built one of the most beautiful – and also one of the wealthiest – of all medieval monasteries. The ruins of Fountains Abbey are vast. The huge church has a fine round-arched nave of the 1160s, a Gothic east end terminating in the Chapel of the Nine Altars and a tall tower added in the late-Gothic style just before the dissolution. Around the cloister, the western range – the lay brothers' quarters – is the most impressive survival, a vast vaulted space. Other buildings where substantial walls survive include the chapter house, monks' refectory and guest houses. Major excavations have also thrown light on other structures, notably the abbey mill.

Freiston Priory
Lincolnshire 1114 Benedictine monks

The largely Norman nave of the priory church survives in parochial use.

Frithelstock Priory
Devon 1220 Augustinian canons

The remains here are of the church and include the east wall, which rises to gable height and has three tall lancet windows. The style of the lancets here and elsewhere suggest that the church was built soon after the priory was founded.

Furness Abbey
Cumbria 1124/1127 Savigniac/Cistercian monks EH

Furness grew to become one of the largest Cistercian monasteries in England, a rival to Fountains. It is still a large site and it is possible to follow the precinct wall around most of it. The outer gatehouse is still the main entrance and the gate chapel is nearby. At the heart of the complex, high walls and rows of pointed Gothic arches and windows

mark the abbey church; nearby the eastern cloister range is especially well preserved, with ruins of the parlour, chapter house and book cupboards. The walls of the infirmary hall survive and the foundations of the kitchen, an octagonal building, can be seen.

Garway Preceptory
Herefordshire c 1185 Knights Templar/Knights Hospitaller

Near the parish church is a round dovecote with truncated cone-shaped roof that belonged to the preceptory of the Templars. Unusually an inscription informs us in Latin that the dovecote was built by Richard in 1326. By this time the house had transferred to the Hospitallers. Nearby an excavation revealed the site of the Templars' round-naved church.

Gisborough Priory
Redcar and Cleveland 1129 Augustinian canons EH

There are few remains here except for the tall eastern wall of the church, with its large window. The gatehouse is nearby.

Glastonbury Abbey
Somerset 601/705 Benedictine monks

This early abbey came to prominence under St Dunstan and became the largest abbey in England. Considering its importance, its ruins are meagre. Most impressive are the fragments of the church, the ornate late Norman chapel of St Mary (which stands as a shell almost to roof height), the superb abbot's kitchen with its tapering stone roof and the abbey gatehouse. In the town are two fine buildings associated with

The Tribunal in the town of Glastonbury was built to house the monastic court.

the abbey: the Tribunal, a court house, and the George, the abbey's pilgrims' inn.

Gloucester Abbey (now Cathedral)
Gloucestershire *c* 679/*c* 1016 Benedictine monks

The abbey of Gloucester came under the Benedictine rule in around 1016, but the oldest parts of the church, which became a cathedral under Henry VIII, are Norman. A large crypt beneath the east end and the nave with its huge round piers are the main survivals from this time. The church was transformed in the 14th century when it became the final resting place of Edward II, who was killed in nearby Berkeley Castle. The east end was remodelled in the new Perpendicular style, with an enormous east window and great 'screens' of stonework concealing the old Norman masonry behind. It is one of the earliest and best examples of this style of architecture in England. The cloisters are of the same period and have the oldest large-scale fan vaults in the country, plus a delightful fan-vaulted washing place. A large number of precinct buildings also survive, many of which are now occupied by the King's School.

Gloucester Blackfriars
Gloucestershire *c* 1239 Dominican friars
EH

This is the best preserved medieval Dominican friary in England and one of only three with substantial

The church at Gloucester Blackfriars still gives the impression of a spacious structure that was designed to attract a large congregation.

remains. The church survives in a truncated form, but enough remains to allow one to appreciate the broad nave for preaching and the narrower chancel. To the south is the cloister with two ranges intact: one containing the refectory, the other a storage room with scriptorium on the upper floor. Much of the masonry is 13th century, though the buildings, especially the church, were much altered after the dissolution, when they were turned into a house. More recently, though, the post-dissolution floors have been removed from the church, so its great space is clear once more.

Gloucester Greyfrairs
Gloucestershire *c* 1231 Franciscan friars
EH

The Greyfriars was extensively rebuilt in the early 16th century and the friary church, which is now

a roofless ruin, survives from this period. The western arm consists of a nave and one wide aisle, creating a generous space for a congregation. No domestic buildings remain.

Godsfield Chapel
Hampshire *c* 1171 Knights Hospitaller

This small 14th-century chapel is what remains of a preceptory of the Knights Hospitaller. The community moved to North Baddesley, near Romsey, in the 14th century, but they left behind a bailiff and a priest, whose house adjoins the chapel.

Godstow Abbey
Oxfordshire 1133 Benedictine nuns

A small building and a walled enclosure marks the site of this Benedictine nunnery north of the city of Oxford.

Grace Dieu Priory
Leicestershire 1239 Augustinian nuns

Fragmentary ruins of this Augustinian nunnery stand in the park of the Victorian Grace Dieu Manor, now a school.

Great Malvern Priory
Worcestershire 1085 Benedictine monks

Apart from the gatehouse, the priory church is the only survival from this Benedictine monastery and it is one of the most interesting of monastic churches. The nave, with its round piers, shows the building's Norman origins. But most of the rest of the

At Hailes the most obvious survival is the cloister with its Gothic arches. Foundations of many of the rooms leading off the cloister also remain.

church dates from the remodelling of 1420–60 in the late medieval Perpendicular style. There is a fine central tower, with panelling and pinnacles, not unlike the one at Gloucester Cathedral, and lots of big windows, many with their original 15th-century stained glass. There is also an outstanding collection of medieval clay tiles, with all sorts of designs – heraldic, animal and abstract.

Hailes Abbey
Gloucestershire 1246 Cistercian monks NT (EH-maintained)

Hailes was a late Cistercian foundation, the result of a benefaction from Richard, Earl of Cornwall, a son of King John. In 1270 Richard's son Edmund presented the abbey with a phial said to contain the blood of Christ.

The square east end of the church was remodelled as a chevet with chapels to provide a fit setting for the precious relic and Hailes became a major pilgrimage centre. Little survives of the church now, but some low walls allow one to trace the domestic buildings and some cloister arches are preserved. Fine carvings, including roof bosses, are preserved in the abbey museum and the nearby medieval parish church may have been the abbey's gate chapel.

Halesowen Abbey
West Midlands 1218 Premonstratensian canons EH

Parts of the buildings were incorporated into a later farm, including the south wall of the church, which is now part of a barn. Other walls of the church, plus cloister buildings, have been incorporated into farm structures.

Hardham Priory
West Sussex 1248 Augustinian canons

The refectory of the priory was converted into a farmhouse that was burned down after the dissolution. Nearby is the ruined chapter house with its beautiful triple-arched entrance, a tantalising fragment.

Haughmond Abbey
Shropshire 1135 Augustinian canons EH

Though founded in 1135, the abbey was substantially rebuilt in the later 12th century. There are substantial remains: the church and cloister walks can be made out largely from their foundations, while features such as the fine chapter house façade, the refectory, the infirmary and the abbot's lodgings have some standing walls.

Hereford Blackfriars
Herefordshire 1322 Dominican friars

Part of the friary was incorporated into a house built after the dissolution and most of the building's details date from after the friars' departure. But a special survival is a 14th-century preaching cross, which stood in the friars' cemetery. It looks like a small hexagonal pavilion with a vaulted canopy and a stone cross in the centre. It is the only such preaching cross to survive in England.

This elegant 14th-century preaching cross in Hereford is a rare survival.

Hexham Priory (now Abbey)

Northumberland 674/1113 Augustinian canons

Originally founded by St Wilfrid, Hexham was refounded for the Augustinians in 1113. Wilfrid's crypt still survives, built of reused Roman masonry, and is one of the two glories of the place. The other is the east end of the church in the beautiful early Gothic style of the late 12th and early 13th centuries. An interesting survival is the night stair in the south transept, which originally linked the church to the canons' dormitory.

Hinton Charterhouse

Somerset 1232 Carthusian monks

Parts of the refectory of this monastery survive and there are traces of the guest house in the later house. However, the main survival here is the chapter house. This is still roofed and has tall gables and lancet windows. The building is in private ownership.

Holm Cultram Abbey

Cumbria 1150 Cistercian monks

Only the six western bays of the abbey church survive to form part of the local parish church. Late 12th-century arches and the western portal are framed by walls and other details of the Georgian period.

Horton Priory

Kent 1142 Cluniac monks

Monastic fragments included in the early 20th-century private house range from the front of the church to the western cloister range. Buttresses, windows, arches and other details from the medieval fabric survive.

Hulne Priory

Northumberland 1242 Carmelite friars

This is the earliest English Carmelite house. It was always a secluded site but is now among the parkland that surrounds Alnwick Castle. There are plenty of remains, including the infirmary, portions of the church and cloister, the chapter house and a tower built in the late 15th century to protect the brothers when there were border troubles.

Hulton Abbey

Staffordshire 1218–20 Cistercian monks

Some of the lower walls of this late Cistercian foundation – notably those of the east end of the church – are visible in the grounds of the adjacent high school.

Hurley Priory

Berkshire 1087 Benedictine monks

The long, narrow nave of this priory church became the parish church. Its windows are Norman with the exception of one 14th-century Gothic one. Nearby to the north, the refectory range is incorporated into a house. To the west of the church a round dovecote and medieval barn may have belonged to the monastery.

Hyde Abbey

Hampshire 901/963/1110 Benedictine monks

A small 15th-century gatehouse is all that remains of Hyde Abbey, an old foundation that became Benedictine in 963 and moved to its site in the middle of Winchester in 1110.

Isleham Priory

Cambridgeshire 1100 Benedictine monks EH

This small Norman chapel with apsidal east end belonged to the alien priory of Isleham. When the alien priories were suppressed, its buildings passed to Pembroke

The church at Isleham was a small plain structure with just a nave and chancel. After the dissolution it was converted to a barn and the large cart door was inserted.

College, Cambridge, in 1440 and the chapel survived as a barn.

Jervaulx Abbey
North Yorkshire 1145/1156 Cistercian monks

This abbey began at Fors in Wensleydale, moving to a site by the River Ure (also known in the Middle Ages as the Jore, giving the place its medieval name of Joreval). There are extensive monastic remains at Jervaulx, including parts of the walls of the 12th-century church and parts of the monks' dormitory and infirmary. The remains of two precinct buildings – a water mill and another building – also survive. The ruins of Jervaulx form part of the park of nearby Jervaulx Hall, where they are maintained and made accessible to the public. The combination of park and ruins makes this one of the most picturesque of English monastic sites.

Kenilworth Abbey
Warwickshire 1125 Augustinian canons

Foundations and fragments of the church and chapter house can be traced, along with two standing buildings: a stone gatehouse and a guest house built of stone, brick and timber.

King's Lynn Priory
Norfolk c 1100 Benedictine monks

An archway and some medieval walls incorporated into later houses mark the site of the Benedictine priory at King's Lynn.

King's Lynn Carmelite Friary
Norfolk 1261 Carmelite friars

A 14th-century gateway of brick and stone formed the entrance to the Carmelite friary in King's Lynn.

King's Lynn Greyfriars
Norfolk c 1230 Franciscan friars

The Franciscans built a church here with a striking octagonal tower of brick and stone. It survives – albeit with a slight lean – together with part of the church it served.

Kingswood Abbey
Gloucestershire 1139 Cistercian monks EH

Kingswood was started as a daughter house of Tintern Abbey but did not find its final site for several decades. The monks ended up in Cotswold sheep country and must have built a fine abbey, but none of it remains except for an early 16th-century gatehouse and small lengths of the precinct wall.

Kirkham Priory
North Yorkshire 1122 Augustinian canons EH

Kirkham was founded by Walter l'Espec, who later founded the more famous Rievaulx Abbey. Excavations have shown the foundations of a series of three churches. The frater, with its vaulted undercroft, and the lavatorium, with beautiful arches, survive from the 13th century. There are also many low-level remains of domestic buildings.

Kirkstall Abbey
West Yorkshire 1147/1152 Cistercian monks

Kirkstall Abbey, a daughter house of Fountains, was one of a number that moved from its first location in its early years. The monks arrived at Kirkstall by the River Aire in 1152 and many of the surviving remains date from the early decades of their settlement. The extensive ruins of the church are still very much of the late 12th century, with many round-headed windows in the Norman style, but also ribbed and pointed vaults in the then new Gothic manner. The only later feature is the crossing tower, which was heightened in the 16th century. The domestic buildings around the cloister are also well preserved, as are the abbot's lodgings. The ruins are now in a public park in Leeds, about 3 miles from the city centre.

Kirkstead Abbey
Lincolnshire 1139/1187 Cistercian monks

Little remains above ground of this daughter house of Fountains, except for one fragment of masonry from the corner of the south transept and some earthworks. The gate chapel, which became a parish church after the dissolution, also survives. It is a beautiful little building of about 1230 or 1240. The chapel is vaulted, with dog-tooth carving on the ribs, and the windows and doorways have shafts with stiff-leaf capitals.

A view from the south transept towards the choir shows the extensive ruins of the church at Lanercost.

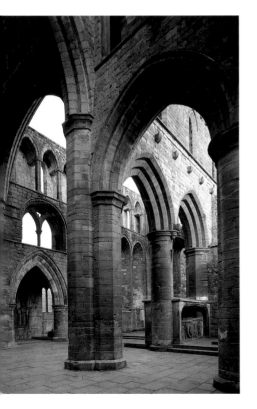

Lacock Abbey
Wiltshire 1232 Augustinian canonesses NT

At the dissolution the cloister buildings were turned into a country house. Many original features remain, including three sides of the beautiful 15th-century cloister and rooms such as the chapter house and sacristy.

Lanercost Priory
Cumbria 1166 Augustinian canons EH

This site contains substantial remains of the Augustinian priory. The church, which is largely early Gothic with many lancet windows, is now in two parts: the ruined east end, which stands almost to roof height, and the nave and aisle, used as the parish church. The eastern cloister range remains only at foundation level, but to the south the refectory undercroft, a long rib-vaulted space, can still be seen. The western range was remodelled as a house at the dissolution, with a tower at one end on the site of the priory kitchen. To the west, a number of precinct buildings probably combine medieval elements with structures built after the dissolution.

Langley Abbey
Norfolk 1195 Premonstratensian canons

The remains of some of the cloister ranges of this abbey were absorbed into a farm after the dissolution. Earthworks in a field beyond mark the site of the church.

Latton Priory
Essex 12th century Augustinian canons

The 14th-century crossing arches of the church are preserved in a large barn, part of Latton Priory Farm.

Leiston Abbey
Suffolk 1365 Premonstratensian canons EH

Substantial remains of the canons' church and cloister range survive. The Lady Chapel, restored and roofed, is still used for worship.

Leominster Priory
Herefordshire 9th century/1123 Benedictine nuns/monks

The Benedictine foundation at Leominster began life as a nunnery. This was dissolved in 1046 and in 1123 the manor was transferred to Reading Abbey, which soon set up the priory again and colonised it with monks. The main survival is the church, now used by the town. Quite a lot of work remains from the period immediately after Reading took over, including the west front with a doorway with carved capitals featuring animals and human figures. Another highlight is the 14th-century south aisle, which has windows encrusted with carved ballflowers, a popular ornament in churches of this period in the west of England. Nothing else survives from the priory except for a nearby building called Priory House, which may have been the monks' reredorter.

Leonard Stanley Priory

Gloucestershire 1121/1146 Augustinian canons/Benedictine monks

This was originally an Augustinian priory that in 1146 was given to the Benedictines of Gloucester Abbey. The church has survived as the parish church and is a solid-looking Norman structure with a central tower and some interesting carved capitals inside. Some of the domestic buildings are incorporated into the neighbouring farm.

Lesnes Abbey

London 1178 Arrouasian canons/Augustinian canons

In Abbey Wood, between Plumstead and Erith in south-east London, stand the ruins of Lesnes Abbey, mostly low walls and foundations.

Lewes Priory

East Sussex 1077 Cluniac monks

This was the first and most important Cluniac monastery in England, but now there is little to show for this history. A few fragments of wall can be seen through fencing on the southern edge of the town.

Lilleshall Abbey

Shropshire *c* 1143 Augustinian canons EH

The remains here include walls of the sizeable church (the Norman west front and Gothic east window are both outstanding), together with cloister buildings including the sacristy, chapter house and refectory.

At the east end of the church at Lilleshall, a 14th-century window has been inserted into the late 12th-century structure.

Limebrook Priory

Herefordshire *c* 1190 Augustinian canonesses

Only a few wall fragments remain of this remote priory of canonesses.

Lincoln Greyfriars

Lincolnshire 1230 Franciscan friars

This long hall with vaulted undercroft is the last standing fragment of the Franciscan friary. It was probably the friars' infirmary.

Lindisfarne Priory

Northumberland 635/1083 Benedictine monks EH

One of our oldest and most famous religious sites, Lindisfarne was originally founded by St Aidan in the 7th century. Viking raids drove the monks away to Durham and the priory was later refounded as a dependency of Durham. Most of the standing remains are early 12th century. The weathered red sandstone ruins include the west front of the church and some nave piers, carved with patterns similar to those at Durham.

Little Dunmow Priory

Essex 1106 Augustinian canons

The south chancel chapel of the former priory is used as the parish church. Inside, close to the north wall, is a row of beautiful moulded arches that originally connected the chapel with the chancel. In the south wall are fine windows that were inserted in around 1360,

Strong defensive walls protect the prior's lodging at Lindisfarne.

below which blind arcading carved with leaves and animals can be seen.

Little Malvern Priory

Worcestershire 1171 Benedictine monks

The priory chancel and tower now make up the parish church and there are ruined portions of the monastic church adjoining. Nearby Little Malvern Court, a private house, incorporates part of the western cloister range.

Llanthony Priory

Gwent 1118 Augustinian canons Cadw

The beautiful ruins of this Augustinian monastery in a remote valley in south-eastern Wales are dominated by substantial remains of the church. A row of nave arches, a large part of the crossing tower and two western towers still stand. One of these towers and the adjoining prior's house were incorporated into a later hotel, which remains. Otherwise virtually nothing survives of the cloister or domestic buildings.

Llanthony Secunda Priory, Gloucester

Gloucestershire 1136 Augustinian canons

There was an Augustinian community at Llanthony in the Black Mountains near the Welsh/English border, but in the 12th century it was threatened and then taken over by the Welsh. The canons sought a safe haven in England and Miles of Gloucester founded a new priory for them in his city in 1136.

Fragments of the priory's outer and inner courts are all that survive today, including part of the outer gatehouse and precinct wall, part of the range between the two courts, part of the brick-built southern range that may have contained stables and the ruins of a large stone barn.

London Bishopsgate, St Helen's

London 1258 Benedictine nuns

The nuns of St Helen's built their church on to an existing parish church, producing a structure with twin naves that remains as the largest parish church to survive the 1666 Great Fire of London. Most of the building as its stands dates from the 15th century.

London Charterhouse

London 1371 Carthusian monks

Parts of the Carthusian monastery, including the entrances to three of the monks' houses, were absorbed into the buildings of the boys' public school.

London Smithfield Priory

London 1123 Augustinian canons

What is now the parish church of St Bartholomew the Great, Smithfield, once belonged to the Augustinian priory. It is London's only example of a Norman church on a large scale, but even so is made up only of the choir and transepts of the original building. The restored eastern cloister walk also survives.

Louth Park Abbey

Lincolnshire 1137/1139 Cistercian monks

This was the home of a daughter community of Fountains. There are few remains except some fragments of masonry and earthworks on agricultural land.

Malmesbury Abbey

Wiltshire 676/970 Benedictine monks

This was one of the most prominent abbeys of the Saxon period, famous as a centre of learning. After various troubles the abbey church was rebuilt in the 12th century and the nave and south porch of this building are still in parochial use. The porch and doorways, decorated with some of the finest carvings of the Norman period, are its chief glory.

Malton Priory

North Yorkshire c 1150 Gilbertine canons

The western part of the Gilbertine church is preserved and used by the parish. There is a fine early Gothic west front of about 1200, with a later medieval window inserted in it. Few domestic remains survive, though the refectory undercroft was incorporated into the nearby Abbey House.

Margam Abbey

West Glamorgan 1147 Cistercian monks

Margam was once the richest Welsh abbey, earning considerable wealth from sheep farming. The main survival is six bays of the nave, which are used as the parish church. It has a well-proportioned west front, basically 12th century though restored in the early 19th century. Nearby are the ruins of the presbytery and the polygonal chapter house.

Mattersey Priory

Nottinghamshire 1185 Gilbertine canons EH

The ruins on this site, once an island formed by the twisting River Idle, include walls of the church, the refectory and a section of the cloister.

Maxstoke Priory

Warwickshire 1337 Augustinian canons

Two gatehouses and parts of the church tower and infirmary survive on private land.

Meare Fish House

Somerset 14th century (abbey foundation c 700) Benedictine monks EH

This small medieval stone building was probably once the house of the water bailiff of Glastonbury Abbey. This structure of the early 14th century has two rooms on the upper floor, which would have been reached by an outer staircase originally. These rooms would have formed the water bailiff's living accommodation while the rooms below were probably used for drying and storing fish.

Meaux Abbey

East Riding of Yorkshire 1150 Cistercian monks

This daughter house of Fountains was founded by William, Count of Aumâle, in recompense for the fact that he had vowed to make a pilgrimage to the Holy Land but had not done so. It survives only as extensive earthworks on agricultural land.

Merevale Abbey

Warwickshire 1148 Cistercian monks

The gate chapel of this daughter house of Bordesley survives as the parish church. It has a small late 13th-century aisled nave and a 15th-century chancel. Little remains of the abbey itself, apart from some walling incorporated in a barn on a working farm.

Michelham Priory

East Sussex 1229 Augustinian canons

Michelham was a small priory but it has left behind some interesting traces. There is a fine 15th-century gatehouse beyond a moat. This leads to a good selection of domestic buildings. The refectory, which was on the south range of the cloister, together with part of the west range, was made into a house after the dissolution and has been preserved by Sussex Past.

Milton Abbey

Dorset 964 Benedictine monks

Parts of the abbey are incorporated into a school, as are the remains of the crossing and the tall and imposing 14th-century Gothic east end of the abbey church.

Minster-in-Sheppey Priory

Kent 670/1087 Benedictine nuns

The building now used as the parish church is actually two churches in one – the northern for the nunnery, the southern for the laity. The southern church is medieval Gothic, but the nuns' church still retains much of its Saxon fabric, an impressive structure with a nave about 50ft (15m) in length. West of the church is the nunnery's other surviving building, a large late medieval gatehouse.

The east wall of the prior's chamber at Monk Bretton has a canopied fireplace that is now well above ground because a floor has vanished.

Monk Bretton Priory

South Yorkshire *c* 1154 Cluniac monks EH

Some of the domestic buildings here are particularly impressive, especially the prior's lodgings, with a well-made fireplace at first-floor level. Gatehouses and a possible courthouse building complete the picture.

Mottisfont Abbey

Hampshire 1201 Augustinian canons NT

Mottisfont is now a large house of the Tudor and Georgian periods. But it is built among the remains of the Augustinian priory (the current name 'Mottisfont Abbey' was the legacy of an 18th-century owner). From the north front, the way the house fits into the priory church can be appreciated.

Mount Grace Priory

North Yorkshire 1398 Carthusian monks EH

This is the best preserved of the English Carthusian monasteries and the remains still clearly show the typical layout of the charterhouse. Around the large cloister are remains of 15 monks' cells, one of which has been reconstructed and furnished. The church survives in ruins with the tower still reaching its full height. There are traces of some of the other buildings and the nearby guest house was converted into a later house.

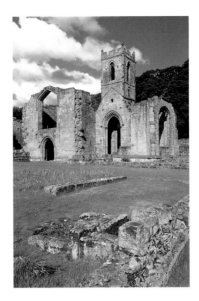

The church at Mount Grace, like most Carthusian churches, is compact, has no aisles and is quite plain.

Muchelney Abbey

Somerset 693/939 Benedictine monks EH

Here the south range of the cloister was remodelled shortly before the dissolution and the abbot's lodgings and part of the refectory make a compact but impressive set of rooms. Inside are interesting decorative touches including a carved fireplace, wall paintings and good ceilings.

The two-storey south cloister range is an important survival at Muchelney Abbey.

Neath Abbey

West Glamorgan 1130 Savigniac/Cistercian monks Cadw

There are substantial remains here of the east and west ranges of the cloister buildings, including a nobly vaulted dormitory undercroft. There are also the remains of a Tudor mansion, built after the dissolution, which incorporates some of the abbot's house. The church is ruined, but fragments of masonry, such as the tall buttresses of the west front, survive to give an idea of its medieval grandeur.

Netley Abbey

Hampshire 1239 Cistercian monks EH

This was a foundation of Peter des Roches, bishop of Winchester. He died while the foundation was being set up and King Henry III gradually took over the role of founder, laying the foundation stone, which can still be seen, and making gifts of land and building materials. The remains include much of the church, cloister and eastern range. The windows of the church show both 13th- and 14th-century tracery designs and in some cases are more ornate than was usual in Cistercian abbeys, perhaps because this was a late foundation.

Newark Priory

Surrey 1189 Augustinian canons

The early Gothic presbytery, the south transept and parts of the north transept of the canons' church are the surviving remains of Newark Priory.

At Blackfriars in Newcastle the south and west cloister ranges have been preserved, though they were much altered when they were taken over by the town's guilds after the dissolution.

Newcastle Austin Friars
Tyne and Wear *c* 1290 Augustinian friars

The 13th-century tower of the friary is the sole survival.

Newcastle Blackfriars
Tyne and Wear *c* 1239 Dominican friars

A courtyard with a number of adapted medieval buildings marks the site of the Dominican friary.

Newenham Abbey
Devon 1247 Cistcerian monks

Scant traces survive of this late Cistcercian abbey. Some medieval stonework is probably incorporated into the walls of farm buildings on private land.

Newminster Abbey
Northumberland 1138 Cistercian monks

This was once a rich daughter house of Fountains, with extensive lands near the Scottish border where sheep were farmed and, apparently, coal was mined. A number of architectural fragments, including parts of the 12th-century cloister, can be found on private but generally accessible land.

Newstead Abbey
Nottinghamshire 1163 Augustinian canons

More properly called a priory, Newstead became well known as Newstead Abbey after it was the home of the poet Lord Byron in the early 19th century. The most magnificent medieval survival is the ornate ruined west front of the church. Other buildings were incorporated into the adjacent house by Byron's ancestors after the dissolution.

Norton Priory
Cheshire 1134 Augustinian canons

The main survival here is the undercroft of the west cloister range, a structure of the late 12th century. The site has been excavated and the foundations of church and cloisters can be seen. The site and museum are administered by a trust.

Norwich Blackfriars
Norfolk 1226 Dominican friars

Now known as St Andrew's Hall this is in fact a unique survival: a complete friars' church consisting of an impressive chancel and a large nave of the kind the friars liked, which housed a sizeable congregation. The church dates to between 1440 and 1470 and is in the Perpendicular style of the time.

Norwich Cathedral Priory
Norfolk 1095–6 Benedictine monks

Beginning as a priory, the Benedictine house at Norwich became a cathedral just five years after its foundation. Its church is still one of the best preserved of all Norman monastic buildings. The cloisters are later but also stunning – they were rebuilt over a long period beginning in 1297 and ending in 1430 and the designs of the walks show how tracery developed through these years. The cloister vaulting is also outstanding, with a superb series of carved bosses showing subjects from the Book of Revelation amongst others. Unusually the cloister has an upper storey, which may originally have been for use in the winter – the space is now used for a library, document store and rooms for the choristers.

Notley Abbey
Buckinghamshire 1162 Augustinian canons

The western cloister range and the abbot's house at Notley were combined after the dissolution to make a house, now in private hands. A medieval square stone dovecote on the rise above the parish church may have belonged to the abbey.

Nun Monkton
North Yorkshire 1153 Benedictine nuns

Part of the church of the nunnery, dating to the 12th and 13th centuries, is in parochial use.

Pentney Priory
Norfolk 1130 Augustinian canons

The large flint-built gatehouse is the sole surviving building of this Augustinian house.

Pershore Abbey
Worcestershire 689/970 Secular canons/Benedictine monks

A truncated abbey church survived in parochial use and even in its abbreviated form, the building is impressive. Part of the nave, the crossing, transepts and chancel still stand; of these, the nave, crossing and transepts are Norman. The chancel was rebuilt in the 13th century – it was consecrated in 1239 – and has beautiful moulded arches and slender lancet windows. This chancel is vaulted and the vault with its pattern of ribs and big carved bosses probably dates from the 1290s.

Peterborough Abbey (now Cathedral)
Cambridgeshire 656/966 Benedictine monks

The former abbey church at Peterborough was made into a cathedral shortly after the dissolution and as a result one of our finest medieval greater churches has been preserved. Much of it is Norman, built after the previous church was damaged by fire in the early 12th century, and the wonderfully regular semicircular arches of the Normans continue through the long nave, into the transepts and through much of the choir. There are elegant Gothic additions at either end – the dramatic arched entrance screen at the west front and an extension of the east end. Remains of the mid-13th-century infirmary survive. The abbot's house forms the core of the bishop's palace, while the guest house became the deanery.

Plympton Priory
Devon 1121 Augustinian canons

A few fragments in the churchyard of St Mary's, Plympton, are testimony to the existence of the priory, once one of the largest English Augustinian houses. There is also a Norman gatehouse nearby.

Prittlewell Priory
Essex 1110 Cluniac monks

The main survival is the two-storey western range (probably the prior's lodging) and the refectory, now used as a museum.

Quarr Abbey
Hampshire 1132 Cistercian monks

Quarr Abbey is on the Isle of Wight. It was originally a Savigniac house and had large estates on the island. At the dissolution most of its stone was removed to build fortifications, but a few fragments remain incorporated into a local farmhouse and barn. There is also a modern Benedictine abbey at Quarr.

Ramsey Abbey
Cambridgeshire 969 Benedictine monks NT

A 17th-century house covers the site of this once-grand abbey. The monastic gatehouse remains intact.

Reading Abbey
Berkshire 1121 Cluniac/Benedictine monks

Henry I founded Reading Abbey and was buried there. The royal connection no doubt helped it acquire the status of an abbey (all other English Cluniac houses were priories), but it is not known why it became a Benedictine house in the 13th century. There are few remains – the site is crossed by the main railway line. The most striking survival is the 13th-century gatehouse.

Reculver Abbey
Kent 669 Benedictine monks

This great Saxon church stood on its coastal site until the early 19th century, when it was demolished by the vicar, who was convinced that it was being used for sacrilegious purposes. The twin west towers were left standing as a guide to shipping. The excavated foundations show the plan of the 7th-century church, which was cruciform and symmetrical with an apse at the east end.

Repton Priory

Derbyshire 7th century/1139 Benedictine
monks/Augustinian canons

There was a Saxon monastery here,
destroyed by the Danes and rebuilt
in the 10th century. The crypt of
this building, with a chancel above,
is preserved as part of the later
church. Parts of the later
Augustinian priory church and
cloister buildings are incorporated
into Repton School.

Richmond Greyfriars

North Yorkshire 1257 Franciscan friars

The 15th-century friary tower is the
important survival here, its
beautiful openwork parapet and
pinnacles making an ornate feature
on the skyline. It is one of a very
few surviving friary towers and has
the friars' typical oblong plan.

Rievaulx Abbey

North Yorkshire 1132 Cistercian monks EH

Rievaulx was the first major
English Cistercian monastery and
its ruins are still some of the most
complete, interesting and evocative
of any English monastic site. Many
of the buildings as they now stand
were the work of Abbot Ailred, who
was head of the monastery between
1147 and 1167. Around 1150 he
rebuilt the church, the transepts of
which survive in part almost to roof
level. The small windows and thick
walls show the austerely elegant
style favoured by the Cistercians at
this time. New cloister buildings
followed and, by the beginning of
the 13th century, the presbytery was

The chapter house at Rievaulx, which survives in the form of low walls, was a rectangular building with an apsidal end.

built in the new Gothic style. The
rows of lancet windows and
moulded arches contrast with the
earlier parts of the church – they
are beautifully proportioned but
still austere. This vast site in its
heyday was home to some 140
monks and around 500 lay
brothers.

Robertsbridge Abbey

East Sussex 1176/1250 Cistercian monks

Fragments of this small monastery
are incorporated into the private
house that now exists on the site.

Roche Abbey

South Yorkshire 1147 Cistercian monks EH

There are substantial remains of
the east end and transepts of the
abbey church at Roche, which

probably date from the late 12th
century. Foundations of the cloister
buildings can be seen, revealing a
typical Cistercian layout. There is
also an infirmary cloister and
various other precinct buildings.
The survival of the ruins is partly
due to the fact that in the 18th
century they became part of a
landscape garden designed by
Lancelot 'Capability' Brown.

Rochester Cathedral Priory

Kent 604/1076 Benedictine monks

Nothing remains to be seen of the
Saxon monastery, though 19th-
century excavations revealed the
foundations of an apsed building
under the cathedral's west front.
This is because the church was
rebuilt under Gundulf, a reforming

bishop appointed in 1076. Gundulf's tower dates from this time and large parts of the building, such as the ornate west doorway, are from slightly later in the Norman period. The east end is in the elegant Early English Gothic of the 13th-century reconstruction. Some of the cloister buildings – adjoining the chancel rather than the nave – survive.

Romsey Abbey

Hampshire 967 Benedictine nuns

The parish church of Romsey originally belonged to the Benedictine nunnery. It is an outstanding structure, dating mainly from the 12th and early 13th centuries and mostly in the Norman style. Tall, round-headed arches rise in the nave to embrace both the arcades and the triforium gallery above, giving the interior noble proportions. It is the best surviving church of an English nunnery.

Rothley Temple

Leicestershire 1231 Knights Templar

The late 13th-century chapel of this house of the Knights Templar is now attached to an Elizabethan and later house. When the Templars were suppressed their buildings passed to the Hospitallers.

Rufford Abbey

Nottinghamshire 1146 Cistercian monks EH

At the dissolution this daughter house of Rievaulx passed to the Talbots, the earls of Shrewsbury. They converted the western cloister range into a house. This preserved one part of the abbey while obliterating much of the rest.

St Albans Cathedral Priory

Hertfordshire c 970 Benedictine monks

A major rebuilding campaign began in about 1077, making St Albans one of the most important early Norman churches. Tall, rather gaunt piers and arches, together with a fine crossing tower, were the result. The masonry has a special appearance because the monks reused bricks and tiles from the old Roman town of Verulamium

At the long abbey church at St Albans, pointed Gothic arches were added in the Middle Ages to the round-headed Norman ones at the eastern end of the nave.

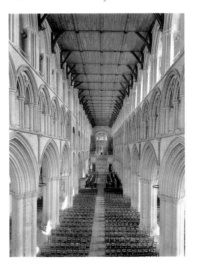

nearby. Little remains other than the church, except for the 14th-century gatehouse.

St Augustine's Abbey, Canterbury

Kent 598 Benedictine monks EH

A complex set of foundations allows the visitor to make out the long history of this important site, which was founded by St Augustine, one of the most influential Christian missionaries to England. This was once one of the greatest Benedictine houses. The outlines of the three 7th-century churches on the site survive, along with later structures including an eight-sided building of c 1050 known as the Rotunda and the large Norman abbey church.

St Benet's Abbey, Ludham

Norfolk 7th century/1019 Benedictine monks

This ancient abbey was refounded in the 11th century by King Canute. Nearly all traces of it have disappeared except for the gatehouse, which survived because it was converted into a windmill.

St Botolph's Priory, Colchester

Essex c 1095 Augustinian canons EH

The priory of St Botolph's was the first Augustinian house in England. No domestic buildings survive but there are substantial remains of the church, including rough circular piers without their facing stone and the arches of a triforium above them. A mixture of stone and reused Roman brick was used in the construction.

St Catherine's Chapel

Dorset 14th century Benedictine monks EH

This stone chapel stands on top of a hill overlooking the village of Abbotsbury. Although small, the chapel is very solidly built and an interior stone vault of the late 14th century shows it to be a high-status building. It was originally a pilgrimage chapel for Abbotsbury Abbey and was later used as a lighthouse.

St Catherine's Chapel at Abbotsbury is a small stone building of the late 14th century.

St Dogmael's Abbey

Dyfed 1113–15 Tironensian monks

The north transept of the church and the infirmary are the main standing ruins of this rare foundation of the Tironensians, an order founded in the early 12th century as a reformed Benedictine congregation. There were several Tironensian monasteries in

Scotland, but few in England and Wales. Their church at St Dogmael's survived in parochial use for a while after the dissolution, but finally fell into disrepair and another church was built nearby.

St Faith's Priory, Horsham

Norfolk 1105 Benedictine monks

Fragments of the medieval buildings were incorporated into a later farm and private house.

St Frideswide's Priory, Oxford
(now Oxford Cathedral)

Oxfordshire 727/late 11th century Benedictine nuns/Augustinian canons

Originally a nunnery, St Frideswide's was refounded for the canons. After the dissolution it became the chapel of Christ Church, one of the largest of the Oxford colleges, a role it still plays as well as being the city's cathedral. It is an outstanding late 12th-century structure with ornate vaulting that was probably added in around 1500.

St George's Priory, Thetford

Norfolk 1160 Benedictine nuns

This was originally home to a community of monks but was refounded in 1160 as a nunnery. Remains of the church still exist on private land among farm buildings.

St Germans Priory

Cornwall 1184 Augustinian canons

The priory church survives in parish use and is complete except

for its chancel, which collapsed in the late 16th century. It is Cornwall's best Norman church, a grand building with two west towers and an enormous portal of seven orders.

St James Priory, Deeping

Lincolnshire 1139 Benedictine monks

The parishioners of Deeping took over the church at the dissolution and it boasts a fine late Norman arcade. The tower – dating from 1730 – is their own addition.

St John's Abbey, Colchester

Essex 1095 Benedictine monks EH

There is not much left of this abbey or of the house that replaced it after the dissolution. The sole important survivor is the gatehouse. This dates from the 15th century and has an outer façade finished in flushwork – the traditional method of making patterns with a mixture of stone and knapped flint.

St John's Commandery, Swingfield

Kent Pre-1180/12th century Sisters of the Order of the Knights of St John of Jerusalem/Knights Hospitaller EH

The site at Swingfield belonged to the Knights Hospitaller. The sisters of the order, who originally occupied it, moved to another site around 1180, after which it became a commandery from which the Knights Hospitaller ran their local estates, using the revenues to fund hospitals for sick pilgrims. The sole surviving building here is the 13th-century chapel, with its beautiful

Part of St John's Commandery survived because it was converted into a farmhouse. Some of the features of the chapel, such as the lancet windows, are still in situ.

timber-framed roof, and part of the adjoining hall.

St Katherine's Priory, Exeter
Devon *c* 1150 Benedictine nuns

A 13th-century building was originally the western range of the cloister of this nunnery. An oak screen inside also dates from the 13th century. Excavations revealed the sites of other buildings around the cloister.

St Leonard's Priory, Stamford
Lincolnshire 658/1078 Benedictine monks

This monastery was originally founded by St Wilfrid and belonged to Lindisfarne, transferring to Durham when the Lindisfarne monks themselves moved there. In the 11th century it was refounded as a cell of Durham. The surviving church is Norman, with a grand-looking but small-scale, west front.

St Mary Magdalene Priory, Lincoln
Lincolnshire *c* 1120 Benedictine monks

The chancel of the church is the remaining fragment of this small cell of St Mary's Abbey in York. It is a 13th-century structure with later windows.

St Mary's Abbey, York
North Yorkshire 1088 Benedictine monks

A few bits of the church, some domestic foundations and substantial parts of the precinct wall with its great gatehouse and towers are the surviving remains of this abbey. A museum preserves many fragments of the building.

St Mary's Priory, Coventry
Warwickshire 1043 Benedictine monks

Only a few fragments remain of this priory, once one of the largest in the West Midlands. The principal surviving parts are some fragments of chapels at the east end of the church, the wall of the west end and part of the base of a tower.

St Nicholas's Priory, Exeter
Devon 1087 Benedictine monks

One wing of the cloister of this small priory near the cathedral survived as a house. Much of it is Norman, with a vaulted undercroft. There is also a guest hall and prior's room, both with good timber roofs.

St Olave's Priory
Norfolk Early 13th century Augustinian canons EH

The remains of the early 13th-century priory of St Olave, an Augustinian foundation, include parts of the church and the 14th-century refectory undercroft. Like several churches in Norfolk, it is dedicated to St Olaf, a king of Norway (died 1030), who converted many Norwegians to Christianity.

St Oswald's Priory, Gloucester
Gloucestershire 1153 Augustinian canons

The Augustinian canons took over a secular collegiate establishment at St Oswald's in 1153. Only the north wall of the original Saxon church, pierced by later arches, remains.

St Osyth's Priory
Essex 7th century/1121 Benedictine nuns/Augustinian canons

The most dramatic survival here is the gatehouse, a dazzling study in flushwork decoration from the 15th century. Patterns of Gothic tracery are picked out in flint and stone above and on either side of the pointed archway. Other remains, including the grand abbot's house built in the early 16th century by Abbot John Vintoner, survive among the various domestic buildings put up by the abbey's post-dissolution owners.

St Paul's Monastery, Jarrow

Tyne and Wear 681/1074 Benedictine monks EH

The nobleman Benedict Biscop founded the monastery at Jarrow and it became famous as the home of the scholar Bede. Though the current church has a 19th-century nave, the chancel is a Saxon structure and a stone gives its dedication date as 23 April 685, making this the earliest known British dedication stone. The remains of the domestic buildings date from after the Norman conquest.

The dedication stone of the church of St Paul at Jarrow is set over the tower arch of the present church. This unique survival probably dates from c 685.

St Radegund's Abbey

Kent 1192 Premonstratensian canons

Remains of the church and cloister buildings, partly incorporated into a farm, survive on private land near Dover.

Sawley Abbey

Lancashire 1146 Cistercian monks EH

This abbey, which began as a daughter house of Newminster, was initially poorly endowed and its lands suffered from a damp climate and poor crop yields. There is quite a large quantity of above-ground remains, mostly quite low, allowing one to trace the shape of the church, with its wide, stubby nave and chancel that was enlarged with the addition of aisles in the 16th century.

Seaton Priory

Cumbria Early 13th century Benedictine nuns

The ruined remains of the early Gothic east wall of the chancel is the only obvious survival of this Benedictine nunnery. The adjacent house – Tudor but much altered in the Victorian period – may incorporate fragments of the monastic buildings.

Selby Abbey

North Yorkshire 1069 Benedictine monks

The imposing Norman and early Gothic church of Selby Abbey became a parish church at the dissolution and remains in use.

Sempringham

Lincolnshire 1131 Gilbertine canons and nuns

This was the home of Gilbert of Sempringham, founder of the Gilbertines, the only native English monastic order. Gilbert began by founding a nunnery for seven women who wanted to take the veil. Later he built a double house for canons and nuns. The parish church consists of the Norman nave and north arcade of the original nunnery church, to which

a later chancel was added in the 19th century.

Shap Abbey

Cumbria 1201 Premonstratensian canons EH

The church's west tower, built probably in the early 16th century, is the main survival at this remote Premonstratensian house. Other fragments allow the visitor to trace the lines of the small church and compact domestic buildings, crammed into a narrow space by the River Lowther.

Sherborne Abbey

Dorset 705/993 Benedictine monks

Sherborne was always an important foundation. It was a monastic cathedral until 1075, when the bishopric moved to Old Sarum. The main survival is the fine church. This is mostly Perpendicular in style because it was largely rebuilt in 1437 after a fire caused during a fight between monks and townspeople. But there are early survivals including some Saxon walling at the west end and some Norman work such as the crossing arches and the south porch. The rest is magnificent Perpendicular Gothic, with huge windows and elegant fan vaults.

Shrewsbury Abbey

Shropshire 1083 Benedictine monks

The nave of the Norman abbey church has survived as a place of parochial worship. This was later extended with a chancel in the 19th century. But the massive piers and semicircular arches of the nave and aisles still give a good idea of the atmosphere and design of the old abbey church.

Shulbrede Priory
West Sussex 1200 Augustinian canons

Part of the refectory and the prior's lodging were converted to a farmhouse after the dissolution. The building was restored in the early 20th century and is well known for its wall painting of the nativity, probably painted after the priory was dissolved.

Sibton Abbey
Suffolk 1150 Cistercian monks

East Anglia's only Cistercian abbey survives only in fragments – parts of the south wall of the nave and the walls of the refectory. The refectory was built on an east–west axis parallel with the nave, rather than on the north–south axis usually favoured in Cistercian monasteries. The ruins are in a wood on private land.

Southwark Priory (now Cathedral)
London 1106 Augustinian canons

The choir, transepts and crossing of the 13th- and 14th-century priory church are still impressive. The nave is a creation of the 1890s, which attempts to recreate the style of the east end.

Stamford Greyfriars
Lincolnshire c 1230 Franciscan friars

The early 14th-century gateway formed the entrance to the Franciscan friary in Stamford. Any of the main friary buildings that survived the dissolution disappeared in the 19th century when the Stamford and Rutland Infirmary was built on the site.

Stanley Abbey
Wiltshire 1151/1154 Cistercian monks

Though there is virtually nothing left of the abbey buildings above ground, Stanley Abbey preserves a good set of earthworks. These encompass the whole abbey precinct, revealing such features as fishponds and a mill as well as the cloister and church. The site is on private land.

Stavordale Priory
Somerset 1263 Augustinian canons

The priory was rebuilt in 1443 and the structure of the church survives because it was converted to a private house after the dissolution.

Stogursey Priory
Somerset c 1100 Benedictine monks

The church of this priory, founded as a cell of the abbey of Lonlay in Normandy, survives in parochial use. Though the church was extended and altered several times during the Middle Ages, a number of Norman arches remain from the original building. Their capitals are vigorously carved with motifs

including animals and a human head, in a style similar to churches across the Channel. The building originally had three apses, a layout also familiar in Normandy.

Stoneleigh Abbey
Warwickshire 1154–5 Cistercian monks

Now well known as the National Agricultural Centre, the site of Stoneleigh Abbey contains remains of the medieval buildings amongst the structure of a house built in the 16th and later centuries. The inner courtyard is based on the cloister and the chapter house and parlour are amongst the surviving monastic rooms. Parts of the church, such as the south wall and part of the south arcade, are also preserved. Many of the remains date from around 1170. Later work is represented by the impressive gatehouse, which was originally built in the 14th century.

Strata Florida Abbey
Dyfed 1164 Cistercian monks Cadw

The ruins of the church, chapter house and parts of the cloister are what remains of the once-important Strata Florida Abbey, a foundation that was well endowed with good lands, becoming a major livestock producer. The abbey suffered several setbacks – in the 13th century there was a lightning strike and fire; in the 14th the buildings were used by troops during Owain Glyn Dwr's uprising, leading to more damage. The most striking fragment of the building that remains is the beautiful west doorway of the church.

Talley Abbey
Dyfed 1184–9 Premonstratensian canons
Cadw

Parts of the crossing and tower are the principle remains at Talley. It was the only house of the Premonstratensian canons in Wales.

Tavistock Abbey
Devon 980 Benedictine monks

Most of the buildings of this town centre abbey have disappeared. The Bedford Hotel is on the site of the refectory and what was probably the infirmary hall became a dissenting chapel. Some fragments of the abbey church wall are visible in the parish churchyard.

Templar Church, Dover
Kent 12th century Knights Templar EH

The foundations of this church, with its round nave and rectangular chancel, were unearthed in the 19th century. The circular nave, together with the location of the church at Dover, the embarkation point for many pilgrims to the Holy Land, suggest that the building may have belonged to the Templars. There were Templars in Dover, but they had probably left by 1185, so the building may have been a small roadside chapel.

The circular foundations of the Templar church at Dover are typical of the order.

Temple Bruer Preceptory
Lincolnshire c 1180 Knights Templar

A tower behind a farmhouse points to the site of a preceptory of the Knights Templar founded towards the end of the reign of Henry II. Excavation showed that there was a typical round Templar church here, but with an unusual east end in which two towers flanked the chancel. It is one of these towers that survives.

Temple Church
London 1162 Knights Templar

The Templars built their first church in London in 1162 and built the round Temple Church a few years later. Though much restored, it is the best surviving example of a circular church of the order. The building's round nave is built in a style transitional between Norman and Gothic, with Norman-style ornamentation and pointed Gothic-style arches. Medieval tombs of crusader knights fill the nave.

A rectangular choir was added in 1220–40.

Tewkesbury Abbey
Gloucestershire 715 Benedictine monks

The church at Tewkesbury is the main survival of one of the great abbeys of the west of England. When the house was dissolved, the people of the town claimed that they already owned the nave and bought the rest of the church, paying £453 to secure one of the finest parish churches in the country. The nave has a magnificent west front with a huge Norman arch; round Norman piers like those at Gloucester are found inside. The big crossing tower, covered with blind arches, is also Norman. The east end of the church is later, dating mainly from a remodelling paid for by the magnate Hugh Despenser and his wife Elizabeth. It contains a superlative collection of late medieval tombs and chantry chapels. To the west of the church are Abbey House, possibly part of the abbot's lodgings, and an early 16th-century gatehouse.

Thame Abbey

Oxfordshire 1140 Cistercian monks

Parts of the abbot's lodgings and other medieval remains survive amongst the structure of the later house of Thame Park, mostly rebuilt in the mid-18th century. The house is privately owned.

Thetford Blackfriars

Norfolk 1335 Dominican friars

Parts of the friars' church including walls of the nave were incorporated into the school later built on the site.

Thetford Priory

Norfolk 1103–4 Cluniac monks EH

Most of the remains here are foundations and low walls, revealing a building similar in layout to Castle Acre. The flint-faced walls of the impressive 14th-century gatehouse stand much higher. A medieval two-storey house known as the Warren Lodge, probably home to the priory's gamekeeper or the keeper of its rabbit warrens, is nearby.

Thorney Abbey

Cambridgeshire 973 Benedictine monks

Part of the abbey church, consisting of seven bays of the Norman nave, was restored and taken over for parish use in the 17th century. The aisles were

This fragment of the chapter house at Thornton Abbey shows the superb quality of its blind tracery decoration.

removed and the Norman arches filled in. An east end was added during the Victorian period.

Thornton Abbey

Lincolnshire 1139 Augustinian canons EH

The main survival here is the magnificent gatehouse, an enormous structure with turrets, an oriel window above the main entrance and arrow slits that make it look like the entrance to some grand castle. The foundations of the church can be seen, plus remains of some of the cloister buildings. The most notable are the two standing walls of the octagonal chapter house, adorned with blind arcading in the style common around 1300.

Thurgarton Priory

Nottinghamshire 1139 Augustinian canons

Parts of the monastic church survive in parochial use. The western section of the nave, a western tower (there were originally two) and a west doorway are the main remains of the 13th-century church.

Tickhill Friary

West Yorkshire c 1260 Austin friars

Two connected ranges of the medieval friary buildings were later converted to houses. Traceried windows and bits of arcading point to remains of the medieval structures.

Tilty Abbey
Essex 1153 Cistercian monks

Tilty Abbey began as a very small site in 1153 and the first major building campaign began towards the end of the 12th century. Only a few fragments of wall survive on the site of the cloister. The parish church is the abbey's gate chapel, which was built in brick as a single-cell building during the 13th century; the chancel was added in the early 14th century.

Tintern Abbey
Gwent 1131 Cistercian monks Cadw

Of all the Cistercian abbeys in striking settings, Tintern, near the River Wye, is perhaps the most beautiful. The church remarkably stands almost to roof level. It dates from the late 13th century, when the foundation expanded and a major rebuilding programme was carried out. The rich window tracery, fine mouldings and ornate doorways show how the Cistercians had left behind their earlier architectural austerity by this time. There are also substantial low-level remains of the cloister and its buildings, unusually placed to the north of the church.

Titchfield Abbey
Hampshire 1232 Premonstratensian canons EH

At the dissolution this abbey was converted into a large house by Sir Thomas Wriothesley, later earl of Southampton. The house was largely pulled down in the 18th century, but some parts remain, such as the enormous gatehouse and parts of the flanking buildings, converted from the nave of the church. A notable monastic survival is the entrance to the chapter house.

Torre Abbey
Devon 1196 Premonstratensian canons

Various survivals here include the abbot's tower, which has a late 12th-century window, a fine tithe barn and a 14th-century gatehouse. Remains allow one to trace the outline of the aisleless church. The entrance to the chapter house, a three-order doorway with openings on either side, can also be seen.

Tupholme Abbey
Lincolnshire 1166 Premonstratensian canons

Fragments of this monastery are dominated by the south refectory wall, with its pulpit and five lancet windows in the style of the early 13th century.

Tutbury Priory
Staffordshire 1080 Benedictine monks

The priory church survived as the parishioners' place of worship, but was largely rebuilt in the 19th century. The glorious west front of the 1160s survives, including the richly decorated doorway, which displays some of the earliest English alabaster carving.

The fine vaulted chapel of the important Percy family adorns Tynemouth Priory.

Tynemouth Priory
Tyne and Wear 7th century/1090 Benedictine monks EH

The Benedictine church had a Norman nave, but the most impressive remains are of the early Gothic east end, where the east and south walls still stand high and imposing, with lancet windows, shafts, dog-tooth mouldings and other decorative details.

Ulverscroft Priory
Leicestershire 1134 Augustinian canons

Ruins including the south wall of the Early English church and part of the cloister survive near a later private house, itself incorporating the prior's lodging.

Vale Royal Abbey

Cheshire 1274 Cistercian monks

Nothing can be seen of the church of this Cistercian foundation. Parts of the cloister buildings may be incorporated into the nearby house.

Valle Crucis Abbey

Clwyd 1201 Cistercian monks Cadw

Substantial ruins survive of this Cistercian abbey, beautifully set in a valley named the Valley of the Cross because of a 9th-century cross commemorating the kings of Powys. The remains include the church, the eastern range of the cloister and foundations of the south and west cloister ranges. A particular highlight is the beautiful vaulted chapter house, which probably dates to the mid-14th century. Above is the monk's dormitory, part of which was later converted to form a hall for the abbot.

Walsingham Priory

Norfolk 1169 Augustinian canons

Fragments of the chancel and domestic buildings – notably the dormitory undercroft, which was absorbed into the later house – are what remain of the medieval priory at Walsingham, built after the lady of the manor had a vision of the Virgin Mary. In the 20th century both the Anglican and Roman Catholic churches built shrines here.

Waltham Abbey

Essex 1177 Augustinian canons EH

The Norman nave and 14th-century Lady Chapel survive in parochial use. The parishioners added a tower in the 1550s, after they had taken over the building. In addition some other remains of this once-great abbey have been preserved – the late 14th-century gatehouse survives, along with part of the cloister's north range and a medieval bridge.

Watton Priory

East Riding of Yorkshire 1150 Gilbertine canons and canonesses

This was the largest Gilbertine priory in England. The main survival is the prior's house, an elaborate building of the 14th and 15th centuries, which must have been more luxurious than many a medieval lord's house. Brick walls and a large, well-decorated bay window of stone make an impressive composition.

Waverley Abbey

Surrey 1128 Cistercian monks EH

This was Britain's first Cistercian monastery. Only fragments of the church survive – however, these reveal that a modest Romanesque structure was replaced by a grander building at the beginning of the 13th century. At this time the monastery was expanding – in 1187 there were some 70 choir monks and 120 lay brothers – and the domestic buildings on the site were also enlarged. In addition, because Waverley was prone to flooding, the monks had to raise the floor level of their buildings at various points, so structures of various dates are visible, revealing to archaeologists the foundations of many of the earlier buildings below the later ones. Amongst the more substantial remains are parts of the eastern cloister range and the south transept of the church.

Wenlock Priory

Shropshire 680/c 1050 Benedictine nuns/Cluniac monks EH

Originally a Saxon nunnery, Wenlock was refounded for the Cluniacs in the mid-11th century. There are impressive remains of the church, with good 13th-century transept walls. Other highlights are the walls of the chapter house, covered in intersecting blind arches in an ornate style favoured by the Cluniacs, and the lavatorium, with

The tall end gable of the south transept gives an idea of the scale of the church at Wenlock Priory.

its beautiful sculptured panels of the late 12th century. The infirmary and fine prior's house were incorporated into a later dwelling nearby.

West Acre Priory

Norfolk 1135 Augustinian canons

Fragments of this once-large Augustinian house stand among farm buildings. The most substantial survivals are the gatehouse, built of flint but with brick patching, and a large barn.

Westminster Abbey

London c 618/959/1050 Benedictine monks EH (part)

One the country's great abbeys, Westminster was rebuilt by Edward the Confessor. The current church is in a mixture of styles – the 13th-century choir and crossing,

Westminster Abbey's nave is beautifully vaulted in the style of the 13th century.

the 14th-century nave and Henry VII's great eastern chapel of the 16th century. The famous two towers of the west front are most recent of all – they were designed by the architect Nicholas Hawksmoor and built in the early 18th century. Cloisters also survive, together with the dormitory, which is now the great hall of Westminster School. The octagonal chapter house, dating to the mid-13th century, was heavily restored in the 19th century, but its elegant ribbed vault and large windows with tracery still make it one of the great monastic rooms.

Wetheral Priory

Cumbria 1106 Benedictine monks EH

Only the gatehouse, with Perpendicular windows, survives of this Benedictine house by the River Eden.

Whalley Abbey

Lancashire 1172/1296 Cistercian monks EH (part)

Though little remains of the church there are quite substantial cloister remains at Whalley together with a good gatehouse of the 14th century. The western range, completed in the 15th century, survives and is roofed. Originally built for the lay brothers, it now houses a chapel. The walls of the ruined eastern range stand quite high, revealing details such as recesses for book cupboards. A vestibule leads to the chapter house, which was octagonal. There are also remains of the separate abbot's house and

The gatehouse of Whalley Abbey is seen from the north. This large building was once the entrance to a precinct of around 200 acres (81 hectares).

infirmary block, with much 15th- and 16th-century work.

Whitby Abbey

North Yorkshire 657/1078 Benedictine nuns and monks EH

Whitby was originally the site of St Hild's double monastery of the Saxon period, but the remains are those of the later Benedictine monastery. The outstanding remains on this coastal site are those of the east end of the church, which was rebuilt in around 1220 with rows of lancet windows.

White Ladies Priory

Shropshire 1199 Augustinian canonesses EH

Minimal remains reveal a late Norman church without aisles. Some of the buildings were converted to a house after the dissolution, but this was later demolished.

Wigmore Abbey

Herefordshire 1179 Augustinian canons

Some late 12th-century wall fragments remain from the church, once the burial place of the

Mortimer family who founded the abbey. Nearby is the late medieval abbot's lodging.

Wilmington Priory
East Sussex 1086 Benedictine monks

This small house was an alien priory. The few monks who lived here used the parish church and did not build a cloister. Instead there was a house of stone, flint and brick, with various rooms that are difficult to interpret but make a picturesque group.

Winchester Cathedral Priory
Hampshire 643/964 Benedictine monks

In the Norman period Winchester was so prominent that it was virtually a second capital city and the city remained important throughout the Middle Ages. Its bishop was one of the most important men in the kingdom and the cathedral-priory was a large and magnificent building. Today the church is the longest in England. The oldest parts are the transepts, where there are early Norman arches and window openings. But much of the church, especially the long nave, was remodelled in the late 14th century in Perpendicular style. The main surviving cloister buildings are the Norman chapter house and the building now known as the Deanery, which began life as the prior's lodgings.

Witham Priory
Somerset 1179 Carthusian monks

Witham was the first Carthusian house in England. It did not thrive until its third prior – later to become famous as Bishop Hugh of Lincoln – took over. His church, much altered but still simple, aisleless and rib-vaulted, survives as the parish church. A monastic dovecote survives in the nearby village.

Woodspring Priory
Somerset 1226 Augustinian canons

Parts of the church of this small Augustinian priory, substantially rebuilt in the years before the dissolution, are incorporated into a later house. The building is now owned by the Landmark Trust and is let as holiday accommodation.

Worcester Cathedral Priory
Worcestershire 7th century/961 Benedictine monks

The cathedral at Worcester is one of several Benedictine churches in the west of England with Norman origins and a Perpendicular central tower – Great Malvern and Gloucester are the two other prime examples. The transepts, crypt, chapter house and refectory are the earliest portions, dating from a building campaign that started in 1084 and continued until the mid-12th century. The east end is mainly 13th century and the nave is mostly from later in the Middle Ages. The building looks stunning on its site above the River Severn, though the exterior owes its appearance to a major Victorian refacing.

Worcester Greyfrairs
Worcestershire c 1227 Franciscan friars NT

The beautiful timber-framed building known as Greyfriars was probably the guest house of Worcester's Franciscan friary. This structure of around 1480 was later converted to a house.

Worksop Priory
Nottinghamshire 1119 Augustinian canons

The Augustinians' Norman nave with its twin west towers is now the parish church. A south transept, built in the 1920s, links it to the canons' Lady Chapel. A fine gatehouse of the 14th century is the other surviving priory building.

Wymondham Abbey
Norfolk 1107 Benedictine monks

The abbey church has survived in parochial use. It looks odd because it has a tower at each end – one with an octagonal top at the east end and a more conventional square one at the west. The eastern tower was originally at the crossing and was built by the monks in about 1400; the parishioners built the west tower in around 1440.

Yarmouth Friary
Norfolk 1271 Franciscan friars

Traces of the cloisters are incorporated into some of the buildings of Great Yarmouth's South Quay.

Glossary

Abbey 1 Large or high-status monastery, presided over by an abbot or abbess; 2 General term for a monastic house

Abbot female form **abbess** Head of an abbey

Alien cell Small monastic house, set up by an overseas monastery, usually to provide a base from which lands could be managed

Alien priory Monastery set up as a British branch or dependency of an overseas abbey

Ambulatory Passage encircling the choir of a church

Anchoress male form **anchorite** Person who adopts a life alone and apart from the world, living in a strictly enclosed anchorage or cell and devoting themselves to prayer

Antiphoner Book containing a collection of chants used in divine service

Apse Rounded or polygonal end to part of a church

Austin canon Member of the Augustinian order

Austin friar Member of the order of friars know as the Hermit Friars of St Augustine

Barrel vault Vault in the form of a continuous half-cylinder; also called a tunnel vault

Bishopric The office of bishop or the geographical area over which he has spiritual and administrative power

Black friar Member of the Order of Friars Preacher, also known as the Dominicans

Black monk Benedictine monk

Blind Term used to describe features, such as arches or windows, that are blocked or blank

Blind arcade Series of decorative blank arches attached to the surface of a wall

Boss Carved stone at the intersection of the ribs in a vaulted ceiling

Breviary Book containing the words, and commonly also the music, for all the divine offices

Buttress Support built against a wall

Cable Type of moulding in the form of a rope; used in Norman architecture

Canonical hours Services sung or recited at eight specific times during the day; also called the divine office

Carrel Small recess or alcove, containing a desk, where a monk could write and study

Cathedral-monastery *See* cathedral-priory

Cathedral-priory Building in which the functions of cathedral and monastery were combined; the bishop normally also took the title of abbot, but the government of the monastery was usually in the hands of the prior; also known as a cathedral-monastery

Cell 1 Small monastic house, normally with accommodation for only a handful of monks or nuns, set up as a branch of a larger monastery; 2 In Carthusian monasteries and some early abbeys, the individual accommodation of a monk or nun; 3 A room set aside for punishment

Cellarer female form **cellaress** Obedientiary in charge of a monastery's stores and supplies of food, fuel and other commodities

Cellarium store room

Cenobitic Term describing the way of life of the monastic community, as opposed to the eremitic life of the hermit

Chancel The eastern section of a church, containing both the choir and presbytery

Chapter Daily meeting of the inhabitants of a monastery, at which matters of discipline and business were discussed and a chapter of the rule was read

Chapter house Room in a monastery in which chapter was held

Checker Room acting as an office, especially an accounting office or counting house

Chevet Design often used for the eastern end of a church, with a rounded apse, ambulatory and, usually, a number of radiating chapels

Chevron Moulding in the form of a zigzag; used in Norman architecture

Choir Area of the eastern part of a church, usually separated from the rest of the building by screens, where the monks gathered to sing or recite the divine office; also called the quire

Claustral prior Disciplinary officer in some monasteries; distinct from the prior, who was the deputy head of an abbey or the head of a priory

Clerestory Row of windows in a church, positioned above the roofs of the aisles to throw light into the nave

Cloister Rectangular courtyard, surrounded by a covered walk, giving access to the main domestic rooms of a monastery and connecting them to the church

Collation Short reading on the monastic life, taking place in the evening either in the chapter house or in one of the walks of the cloister

Compline The eighth and last of the canonical hours, taking place before the monks or nuns retired for the night and so ending the monastic day

Conversus In the Cistercian order, a layman who has joined the monastery to serve God with work and prayer; the *conversi* were monks, in that they followed the rule, but they said a shorter form of the office than the choir monks and devoted their lives to manual work rather than to study; also known as lay brothers

Corbel Block projecting from a wall, designed to support some other structural element

Corrodian Person who paid a monastery in money or goods, or left their estate to a monastery, in return for food and accommodation until they died

Crocket Decorative stone, usually carved to resemble a leaf, adorning features such as spires or pinnacles on medieval churches

Cruciform Cross-shaped

Daughter house Monastery founded by sending out a group of monks or nuns from another abbey (the parent house) to start a new monastic community

Day stair Stairway, usually next to the chapter house, linking the cloister with the dormitory

Decorated Second phase of English Gothic architecture fashionable in England in the late 13th and 14th centuries and characterised by more lavish ornament than in Early English architecture

Demesne Portion of an estate that the landlord, for example a monastery, kept in its own hands, and which was farmed by its own workers or monks

Dependent house Monastery that is a subsidiary or cell of another religious house

Diocese Geographical area over which a bishop holds spiritual and administrative power; also known as a see

Divine office The canonical hours – the services sung or recited at eight specific times during the day – or one of these services

Dog-tooth Decorative motif consisting of a repeated four-pointed star-like design; used in Gothic architecture

Dormitory Room in which monks or nuns slept; also called the dorter

Dorter *See* dormitory

Early English First phase of English Gothic architecture, fashionable mainly in the 13th century and typified by features such as simple lancet windows

Eremitic Term describing the solitary way of life of the hermit, as opposed to the communal, or cenobitic, lifestyle of the monk or nun

Fan vault Type of stone-vaulted ceiling featuring ornate cone-shaped masses of stone, fashionable in the 15th and 16th centuries

Flying buttress Arch-like structure on the outside of a building, transferring the thrust of a heavy vaulted ceiling to a substantial outer support

Frater *See* refectory

Friary Religious house occupied by members of one of the orders of friars

Garderobe Medieval privy or lavatory

Garth The courtyard of a cloister, usually occupied by a lawn or garden

Gate chapel Chapel at or near the gate of the monastery, mainly for the use of visitors to the abbey

General chapter Meeting of the heads or representatives of all the monasteries of a particular religious order

Grange Farm belonging to a monastery but usually some distance away from it, which was run by the monks and worked by servants or lay brothers

Grey friar Member of the Order of St Francis

Groin vault Vault in which surfaces meet at a pronounced edge without structural ribs

Guest master Obedientiary responsible for the accommodation and welfare of the abbey's guests

Habit Clothing worn by a monk or nun

Holy See The papacy

Infirmarer Obedientiary responsible for running the abbey's infirmary

Kitchener Obedientiary responsible for overseeing the kitchen, supervising the cooks, selecting food and related matters

Lady Chapel Chapel, usually in the easternmost portion of a church, dedicated to the Blessed Virgin Mary and where Masses in her name were celebrated

Lancet Tall, narrow window with a pointed head, common in 13th-century architecture

Lantern Open or glazed turret at the top of a roof or dome

Lauds A short service that was celebrated jointly with matins, so that the combined office was sometimes referred to as 'matins and lauds'

Lavatorium *See* laver

Laver Monks' or nuns' washing place

Lay brother *See conversus*

Lectionary Book containing selections from the Bible, for reading aloud during divine services

Light One section of a window, separated from the others by vertical mullions

Limitor Person who begged on behalf of mendicant friars, making a profit in the process

Louver Opening in a roof to allow smoke from a fire to escape

Matins The second of the canonical hours, taking place at daybreak

Mendicant Person, especially a friar, who relies on alms for survival

Misericord or **misericorde** 1 Hinged seat with a protruding ledge, designed to give support to the user while standing; 2 A relaxation of certain monastic rules, especially for monks or nuns who were elderly or sick

Missal Book containing the words and instructions for the celebration of Mass throughout the year

Moulding Ornamental carving applied to the projecting sections of an arch, doorway, window, wall or other architectural feature

Mullion Vertical post or stone bar dividing a window into separate lights

Nailhead A form of ornament used in early Gothic architecture consisting of a band of repeated small pyramids

Nave Western section of a church, used either by lay worshippers in an abbey church or, in the Cistercian order, by the lay brothers

Night office *See* nocturns

Night stair Stairway connecting the dormitory with the church, allowing the monks or nuns easy access to church for the night office

Nocturns The first of the canonical hours, sung in the middle of the night; often referred to as the night office

None The sixth of the canonical hours, sung before the inhabitants of the monastery had lunch

Novice Monk or nun serving a training and probationary period before being fully accepted into the monastic community

Novitiate Period of probation and training undergone by a novice

Obedientiary Monk or nun with responsibility for a specific aspect of the running of the monastery; for example, the cellarer, kitchener or infirmarer

Oblate Child given to a monastery by their parents, to be brought up as a member of the religious house

Office *See* divine office

Ogee Double-curved line or arch made up of both concave and convex curves

Order Community of monks or nuns making up a body following a specific religious rule and usually united by an overall organisational structure

Parent house Monastery from which one or more subsidiary (or daughter) houses have been founded

Parlour Room in a monastery in which the usual rule of silence was relaxed; many monasteries had two parlours: one for the use of members of the monastic community and one in which the monks or nuns could meet with outsiders

Perpendicular Third and final phase of English Gothic architecture, popular in the 15th century and characterised by straight verticals and fan vaulting

Pier Solid masonry support or pillar

Pittance Addition to the usual monastic diet, usually given to mark a saint's day or other feast

Poor Clares Female members of the Order of St Francis, also known as Minoresses or members of the Second Order of St Francis

Porticus Side chamber in a Saxon church, leading off the nave

Postulant Person seeking to be admitted to a monastic order

Potence Ladder mounted on a revolving mechanism, designed to give access to the nesting holes in a dovecote

Precentor Obedientiary in charge of all the music used in an abbey

Precinct The area of land on which a monastery and its buildings stood, usually protected by a boundary wall or fence and entered through one or more gatehouses

Presbytery The easterly area in a monastic church, east of the choir, where the high altar was situated

Prime The third of the canonical hours, sung or recited in the early morning

Prior female form **prioress** 1 In an abbey, the deputy head (or, when called the claustral prior, the monk in charge of discipline); 2 In a priory, the head of the monastery

Priory A monastery led by a prior or prioress

Psalter Book of psalms

Pulpitum Screen at the western end of the choir, separating the part of the church used by the monks from that occupied by the laity

Quire *See* choir

Reeve Lay official placed in charge of a manor to supervise the workforce

Refectory Monks' communal dining room; also known as the frater

Regular canon Member of the clergy who follows a monastic rule

Reliquary Container holding sacred relics

Reredorter Building containing the principal latrines in a monastery

Reredos Decorative screen rising behind the high altar

Scriptorium Room or area in a monastery where the monks or nuns wrote or copied manuscripts

Scrutator In the Gilbertine order, inspector who visited each monastery annually

Secular canon Member of the clergy attached to a cathedral or collegiate church and not following a monastic rule

See *See* diocese

Sext The fifth of the canonical hours, recited or sung in the middle of the day

Shaft Small column, often placed on either side of a doorway or window

Slype Passage, usually running off the eastern cloister walk and giving access to buildings such as the monastery's infirmary

Stiff leaf Form of stylised carved foliage, fashionable in the architecture of the early-13th century and often used on the capitals at the tops of pillars and also on roof bosses

Terce The fourth of the canonical hours, recited or sung in the morning before the first Mass of the day

Tracery Decorative pattern of stonework in the upper portion of a window

Transept Northern and southern projecting arms of a church, usually containing chapels in which those monks who were also priests could celebrate Mass

Transom Horizontal stone bar dividing up a window

Transubstantiation Doctrine that the bread and wine taken at Mass alter in substance during the rite, becoming the actual body and blood of Christ

Triforium Gallery above the aisle of a church, overlooking the nave

Tympanum Semicircular panel above a doorway, often carved with a relief panel

Undercroft Vaulted room either below ground or below a main room

Vault Ceiling built of stone or other masonry

Vespers The seventh of the canonical hours, recited or sung after the afternoon work session

Walking space Area between the choir and the nave in a friary church

Warming house Room in a monastery where a fire was kept lit and where monks or nuns were allowed to go to get warm, especially when they were undertaking cold, sedentary work in the scriptorium

White canon Member of the Premonstratensian order

White friar Member of the order of Our Lady of Mount Carmel, known as the Carmelite friars

White monk Member of the Cistercian order

Further reading

The following is a small selection of the many books on medieval British monasteries. Most have extensive bibliographies, which will enable readers to follow up specific interests.

Aston, M 2000 *Monasteries in the Landscape*. Stroud: Tempus

Bond, J 2004 *Monastic Landscapes*. Stroud: Tempus

Brooke, R B 1975 *The Coming of the Friars*. London: George Allan and Unwin

Carver, M (ed) 1993 *In Search of Cult*. Woodbridge: Boydell Press

Colvin, H M 1951 *The White Canons in England*. Oxford: Clarendon Press

Coppack, G 1990 *English Heritage Book of Abbeys and Priories*. London: Batsford

Coppack, G 2000 *The White Monks: The Cistercians in Britain 1128–1540*. Stroud: Tempus

Coppack, G and Aston, M 2002 *Christ's Poor Men: The Carthusians in Britain*. Stroud: Tempus

Farmer, D H and Stockdale, R (eds) 1980 *The Benedictines in Britain* (British Library Series no. 3). London: The British Library

Forey, A 1992 *The Military Orders: From the 12th to the early 14th centuries*. London: Macmillan Education

Golding, B 1995 *Gilbert of Sempringham and the Gilbertine Order c 1130–c 1300*. Oxford: Clarendon Press

Greene, J P 1992 *Medieval Monasteries*. Leicester: Leicester University Press

Knowles, D 1948, 1955, 1959 *The Religious Orders in England* (3 vols). Cambridge: Cambridge University Press

Knowles, D 1950 *The Monastic Order in England*. Cambridge: Cambridge University Press

Lawrence, C H 1984 *Medieval Monasticism: Forms of religious life in Western Europe in the Middle Ages*. London: Longman

Lawrence, C H 1994 *The Friars: The impact of early mendicant orders on Western society*. London: Longman

Morris, R 1979 *Cathedrals and Abbeys of England and Wales: The building church, 600–1540*. London: Dent

Platt, C 1984 *The Abbeys and Priories of Medieval England*. London: Secker and Warburg

Robinson, D M 1980 *The Geography of Augustinian Settlement in Medieval England and Wales* (BAR British series 80). Oxford: British Archaeological Reports

Robinson, D M (ed) 1998 *The Cistercian Abbeys of Britain: Far from the concourse of men*. London: Batsford

Thompson, S 1991 *Women Religious: The founding of English nunneries after the Norman Conquest*. Oxford: Clarendon Press

Youings, J A 1971 *The Dissolution of the Monasteries*. London: George Allen and Unwin

Acknowledgements

The author would like to thank the army of people who look after and interpret the monastic remains of England and Wales and who have helped to make the years of travelling and ruin-visiting that preceded the writing of this book such a pleasure. In addition, thanks to: John Brooks, Zoë Brooks, David Johnston, Marion Scott and James Wingate, for help and answers to questions; Sugra Zaman for encouragement and support; Val Horsler for her initial faith in the project; George Hammond for his exemplary design; Javis Gurr and Nigel Wilkins for their help with the sourcing of images; and the team at English Heritage, especially René Rodgers, for all their hard work.

PICTURE CREDITS

Unless otherwise stated images are © English Heritage.

Other illustrations reproduced by kind permission of: © Peter Ashley: 161; © Jonathan Bailey: 169t; Bridgeman Art Library: 59, 61 & 66 (Huntington Library and Art Gallery, San Marino, CA, USA), 119 (Glastonbury Abbey, Somerset, UK); The British Library: 19 (Arundel 155, f.133), 101 (Add. 42130, f.166v), 152 (Add. 42130, f.176v); © John Critchley: 48, 82, 200; © Crown copyright.NMR: 7, 71, 96, 150t, 193; © Department of Archaeology, Durham University/Photographer T Middlemass: 196; EDIFICE/www.edificephoto.com: 133; English Heritage.NMR: 25, 27, 37, 55, 76, 84, 87, 113r, 118, 140, 150, 160, 168, 202b; © Paul Highnam: 83, 103t, 181; Images of England: 41 (© Mr Jeff Andrews), 183 (© Dr Derek Foxton), 139 (© Mr Robert Hornyold-Strickland), 163 (© Mr Malcolm Osman ABIPP), 148 (© Helmut Schulenburg); www.graeme-peacock.com: 16, 22b, 164, 190; The Trustees of St Augustine's Foundation: 100; © Andrew Tryner: 156; © John Wyand: 64, 88, 98.

Every effort has been made to trace copyright holders and we apologise in advance for any unintentional omissions or errors, which we would be pleased to correct in any subsequent edition of the book.

Index

Numbers in **bold** indicate illustrations; numbers in *italic* indicate entries in the Gazetteer.